PN
57
.C25
M3
1967

Matthews, Honor.
    The primal curse; the myth of Cain
and Abel in the theatre. New York,
Schocken Books [1967]
    221 p. illus. 23 cm.

THE PRIMAL CURSE
THE MYTH OF CAIN AND ABEL IN THE THEATRE

To
M

By the same Author

CHARACTER AND SYMBOL IN
SHAKESPEARE'S PLAYS

1. Cain and Abel: from the Holkham Bible Picture Book.
English; second quarter of the 14th century.

THE
PRIMAL CURSE

The Myth of Cain and Abel
in the Theatre

By

HONOR MATTHEWS

SCHOCKEN BOOKS · NEW YORK

Published in U.S.A. in 1967
by Schocken Books Inc.
67 Park Avenue, New York, N.Y. 10016

Library of Congress Catalog Card No. 67–11107

Printed in Great Britain

CONTENTS

ILLUSTRATIONS

ACKNOWLEDGEMENTS

I am grateful to the following for permission to quote from copyright material:

Atheneum Publishers (for Edward Albee's *Who's Afraid of Virginia Woolfe*); John Calder Ltd. (for Samuel Beckett's *How It Is*, and Eugene Ionesco's *Plays*, Vol. II); Jonathan Cape Ltd. (for August Strindberg's *Road to Damascus*, translated by Graham Rawson, and Arnold Wesker's *Chips with Everything*); Chilmark Press Inc. (for David Jones's *The Anathemata*); Collins-Knowlton-Wing Inc. (for August Strindberg's *Dream Play, The Father, Ghost Sonata* and *Miss Julie*, all translated by Elizabeth Sprigge); Coward-McCann, Inc. (for Edward Albee's *The Zoo Story*); The Dial Press Inc. (for James Baldwin's *The Fire Next Time*); Doubleday & Co. Inc. (for *The Wakefield Mystery Plays*, edited by Martial Rose, and Martin Esslin's *Brecht*); Editions Gallimard (for Samuel Beckett's *Comment C'Est*, Albert Camus's *Le Mythe de Sisyphe* and Jean-Paul Sartre's *Saint Genet*); Grove Press Inc. (for Samuel Beckett's *Endgame, Happy Days* and *Waiting for Godot*, Bertolt Brecht's *Baal*, translated by Eric Bentley and Martin Esslin, and *Mother Courage*, translated by Eric Bentley, and Hugh Kenner's *Samuel Beckett*); Grove Press and Rosica Colin Ltd. (for Jean Genet's *The Blacks, Death Watch* and *The Maids*, all translated by B. Frechtman); Hamish Hamilton Ltd. (for Albert Camus's *Caligula and Cross-Purpose*, translated by Stuart Gilbert, and Jean-Paul Sartre's *The Flies*, translated by Stuart Gilbert, *Loser Wins*, translated by S. and G. Leeson, and *Three Plays*, translated by K. Black); Hammond, Hammond & Co. (for Henrik Ibsen's *Peer Gynt*, translated by Norman Ginsbury); Harcourt, Brace & World Inc. (for 'The Hollow Men' from T. S. Eliot's *Collected Poems 1909–1962* and 'Little Gidding' from his *Four Quartets*); Harper & Row Inc. (for Mircea Eliade's *Myths, Dreams and Mysteries*); Heinemann Educational Books Ltd. (for Henrik Ibsen's *Brand*, translated by J. Forsyth); David Higham Associates Ltd. (for Dante's *Divine Comedy*, translated by Dorothy Sayers, and August Strindberg's *When We Dead Awaken*, translated by M. Meyer); Indiana University Press (for Mark Spilka's *Dickens and Kafka*); Alfred A. Knopf Inc. (for Franz Kafka's *The Castle* and *The Trial*, both translated by Edwin and Willa Muir, and Thomas Mann's *Dr. Faustus*, translated by H. T. Lowe-Porter); Van Loewen Ltd. (for Julian Green's *South*); Methuen Ltd. and Grove Press (for John Arden's *Serjeant Musgrave's Dance*, and Harold Pinter's *The Collection* and *The Dumb Waiter*); Oxford University Press (for Christopher Fry's *Sleep of Prisoners*); Pantheon Books Inc. (for Denis de Rougemont's *The Myths of Love*); Penguin Books (for Henrik Ibsen's *Hedda Gabler and Other Plays* and *The Master Builder and Other Plays*, all translated by Una Ellis-Fermor); Princeton University Press (for Sören Kierkegaard's *Concept of Dread, Concluding Unscientific Postscript* and *Fear and*

Trembling, all translated by W. Lowrie); Routledge and Kegan Paul Ltd. (for C. G. Jung's *Psychology of the Unconscious*, translated by N. Hinkle); Charles Scribner's Sons (for Martin Buber's *I and Thou*, translated by R. G. Smith); Sheed & Ward (for Mircea Eliade's *Images and Symbols* and *Patterns in Comparative Religion*); the S.P.C.K. and Harper & Row Inc. (for *Kerygma and Myth*, translated by R. H. Fuller); St. Martin's Press Inc. (for John Wain's *Weep Before God*); University of Kentucky Press (for Robert Heilman's *Magic in the Web*); University of Notre Dame Press and the Clarendon Press, Oxford (for Beryl Smalley's *The Study of the Bible in the Middle Ages*); Vanguard Press Inc. and David Higham Associates Ltd. (for Edith Sitwell's 'Ass-Face'); A. P. Watt & Son and Trinity College, Cambridge (for Sir J. Frazer's *Folklore in the Old Testament*); A. P. Watt & Son (for Dante's *Inferno*, translated by Dorothy Sayers); The World Publishing Co. and Faber & Faber Ltd. (for Martin D'Arcy's *The Mind and Heart of Love*); and Yale University Press (for Eugene O'Neill's *Long Day's Journey into Night*, and Ernst Cassirer's *Philosophy of Symbolic Forms*).

A NOTE ON THE TEXTS CITED

The Shakespearean quotations are from the Folio text as printed in the New Nonesuch Shakespeare 1929. The spelling has been modernised by the author.

In the case of Ibsen's plays, quotations from *Brand* and *Peer Gynt* are from versions respectively by J. Forsyth and N. Ginsbury which have been successfully used on the stage in recent years. Otherwise the translations used are by Una Ellis-Fermor where these exist. *When We Dead Awaken* is quoted in the translation by M. Meyer.

Where paper-back editions of plays and other works are available those editions are those referred to in the text, as it is hoped this may be useful to the general reader.

Part I

THE
MYTH OF CAIN AND ABEL
IN THE THEATRE OF AN
ORDERED SOCIETY

For the Word came into the world by Mary, clad in flesh;
knowledge of the divinity was given to the chosen few. So
when the Word was shown to men through the lawgiver
and the prophets, it was not shown them without suitable
vesture. There it is covered by the veil of flesh, here of the
letter. The letter appears as flesh; but the spiritual sense
within is known as divinity . . . Blessed are the eyes which
see divine spirit through the letter's veil.

From Origen, *Homilae in Leviticum*

It is a mark of Cain in our culture that we have no symbols
any more and—worse—that we are unable to create them.

Oskar Schlemmer, from *The Theater of the Bauhaus*,
by Schlemmer, Maholy-Nagy and Molnar

Tragedy imposes a noble parable, *myth*, between the
universality of its music and the . . . spectator . . . [With-
out myth] every culture is dispossessed of its natural,
healthy and creative force; only a horizon constellated
with myths completes the unity of a cultural epoch.
Myth alone can preserve the faculties of the imagination
from the incoherence of a purposeless activity . . .

Nietzsche, *The Birth of Tragedy*

CHAPTER 1

VENGEANCE IS MINE

i. INTRODUCTION

Which blood like sacrificing Abel's cries
(Even from the tongueless caverns of the earth)
To me for justice and rough chastisement.

(Richard II, I. i.)

FROM the choric drama of Athens to the contemporary
'Theatre of the Absurd'; from the exemplary plays of the
Middle Ages to the 'naturalism' of the nineteenth century,
dramatic art has been concerned to reflect men's consciousness
of guilt, fear of punishment and hope of redemption. The roots
of the need to employ fictional representations of such obses-
sional interests are traced by anthropologists into the earliest
stages of cultural development. Mircea Eliade, for example,
points out the value attached by primitive peoples to repeated
presentations of the stories which they believe contain the
truth of the beginning of their world, and what he says is
clearly relevant to the development of our own theatrical
tradition. Of the origins of myth he writes:

> . . . the savage took pains not to forget what had come to pass *in
> illo tempore*. Periodically he re-memorised the essential events
> which had placed him in the position of 'fallen man'. . . . for the
> primitive there are two categories of events taking place in two
> kinds of Time which are qualitatively irreducible: one of these com-
> prises the events we call mythical, which took place *ab origine* . . .
> and all this he must memorise. . . . Periodically the most important
> events were re-enacted and so re-lived. The Remembrance, re-
> enacted ritually—therefore, by the repetition of the primordial
> assassination—plays the decisive part . . . To the primordial myth
> belongs the conservation of the true History, the history of the

11

human condition: it is in this that one must seek and find again the principles and the paradigms for all the conduct of life.* (pp. 44–6)

The story of Cain and Abel is such a primordial myth. Sir James Frazer has shown the extent of the geographical distribution of the story of the two fighting brothers through Europe, Asia, Africa and Polynesia.

The mark of Cain may have been a mode of disguising a homicide or of rendering him so repulsive or formidable in appearance that his victim's ghost would either not know him or at least give him a wide berth. . . . We may suppose that, when Cain had been marked by God, he was quite easy in his mind, believing that the ghost of his murdered brother would no longer recognise or trouble him. What the mark was which the divinity affixed to the first murderer for his protection, we have no means of knowing . . . For example he may have painted him red all over like a Fijian; or white all over like a Ngoni; or black all over like an Arunta; or one half of his body red and the other half white like the Masai and the Nandi. Or if he confined his artistic efforts to Cain's countenance, he may have painted a red circle round his right eye and a black circle round his left eye in the Wogogo style; or he may have embellished his face from the nose to the chin, and from the mouth to the ears, with a delicate shade of vermilion after the manner of the Tinneh Indians. Or he may have plastered his head with mud, like the Pimas, or his whole body with cow's dung like the Kavirondo. Or again, he may have tattooed him from the nose to the ears, like the Eskimo, or between the eyebrows, like the Thonga, so as to raise pimples and give him the appearance of a frowning buffalo. Thus adorned, the first Mr. Smith—for Cain means Smith—may have paraded the waste places of the earth without the least fear of being recognised and molested by his victim's ghost.†

Eliade when discussing the myths of man's original 'fall' to his present condition places among them the story of the

* *Myths, Dreams and Mysteries*, Harvill Press, 1960; originally published as *Mythes, Rêves et Mystères*, Gallimard, 1957.
† *Folklore in the Old Testament*, Sir James Frazer, Macmillan, 1923, p. 45.

original murder. He states that according to the mythology of 'the earliest cultivators of tubers . . . man became what he is today—mortal, sexual and condemned to labour—in consequence of a primordial murder'. He continues: '*In illo tempore* a divine Being . . . consented to be immolated in order that the tubers of the fruit trees might grow from his or her body.' * Although this agrees with the medieval typological interpretation of Abel as a type of Christ, who did indeed consent to his death for the people, yet in the Genesis narrative the story of Cain and Abel is concerned not with redemption but with punishment, and Abel's blood calls from the ground for vengeance on the murderer. Moreover, in Genesis the killing is a result not a cause of the 'fall' of man. It is possible, however, that we have following each other as cause and effect two incidents which in their origins were complementary and concurrent rather than consecutive. The fall in the Garden of Eden follows the eating of the apple of love; the fault is sexuality and it is directly laid to the charge of the woman. In the second story the fault is aggression and it is committed by a man. Eliade quotes an Abyssinian song which runs: 'She who has not yet given birth, let her give birth; he who has not yet killed, let him kill', and continues: 'It is a way of saying that the two sexes are condemned each to accept its destiny.' †

Such levels of meaning, however, have long been forgotten by the conscious minds of Europeans, and in historic times the story of the first murder and its consequences has been related to the search for the balance between deed and consequence which men call justice. The treatment of the story of Cain and Abel is an example of men's prepossession with this search, for, although in the original version punishment of Cain was expressly forbidden, in later re-tellings his crime was inextricably entangled with the Mosaic law of an eye for an eye and a life for a life, 'that kind of wild justice' with which Francis Bacon identified revenge.

Since the story of Orestes was given dramatic form in the

* *Myths, Dreams and Mysteries*, p. 45.   † Ibid., pp. 46–7.

theatre of Dionysus at Athens, audiences have continued to react with peculiar satisfaction to the spectacle of a conflict to the death between two human beings, followed by either a resolution or a renewal of such a conflict. Death, accepted as an absolute breach of the established order, is awaited with suspense, and the accomplishing of the threat of death leaves an imaginative void, the filling of which is awaited with an equal suspense. Where the disruption of order is realised to be 'wrong', the re-establishment of order is felt as a moral necessity of great importance, and the earliest method of achieving such a new balance was the payment of a price equivalent to the destruction caused; in the case of individual murder therefore it was both imaginatively and morally satisfying that a life should be exacted for a life taken. The ceremonial re-enactment of this pattern in theatrical terms is one of the basic forms of what European man calls Tragedy, and the theatre is still concerned to reflect his paradoxical demand that violence be both condemned as unethical and also accepted as the means by which the guilt which the violence leaves in its trail be purged.

In all epochs dramatists are concerned to hammer out in their art acceptable symbols for the basic faith of the society they serve. A belief that human society is part of a universe in which order is assured by the might and beneficence of its Creator may legitimately be reflected in an assumption that men are assured of their deserts. Even where faith in a divinely ordered universe has been shaken, many have continued to believe both in the possibility and in the desirability of such justice and have sought it with fervour: when however a sense of order in the universe is not merely shaken but ceases to exist, and when, in the resulting chaos, men see themselves as flotsam without recognisable obligations or hopes of due reward, then justice becomes a chimera. Whereas in the first case its achievement can be expected as a token of the ordered world, in the second its absence is an equally clear emblem of an 'absurd' or irrational universe.

Although we are not so accustomed as our ancestors to

thinking by means of types and images, yet the importance of metaphorical and symbolic language still remains.

For one of the efficient causes of which the effect called poetry is a dependant, involves the use of language . . . at an especially heightened tension. The means or agent is a veritable torcular, squeezing every drain of evocation from the word forms of that language. . . . And that involves a bagful of mythus before you've said Jack Robinson—or immediately after. . . . All this holds good whether the poet practises his art in some 'bardic' capacity . . . in an early and simple phase of culture (the 'morning' . . .) or whether he happens to be a person who . . . writes poetry in a late and complex phase of a phenomenally complex civilisation (the 'lengthening shadow' . . .) the many amenities of which you and I now enjoy.*

In the Christian societies of Europe the earliest theatrical presentations of justice in the ordered universe are to be found in the medieval Miracle Plays. They familiarised men with types and symbols which passed into the secular drama and remained powerful until, in the seventeenth century, belief in the Christian framework of society weakened, and the theatre came to reflect a world in which faith in a moral order was reduced to a faith in the destructive quality of evil.

The first murder in Christian mythology is told in Genesis IV, and is dramatised in the medieval cycles.

And Cain talked with Abel his brother: and it came to pass when they were in the field, that Cain rose up against Abel his brother and slew him.

And the Lord said unto Cain, Where is Abel thy brother? And he said, I know not; Am I my brother's keeper?

And he said, What hast thou done? the voice of thy brother's blood crieth unto me from the ground.

And now art thou cursed from the earth, which opened her mouth to receive thy brother's blood. When thou tillest the ground, it shall not henceforth yield unto thee her strength, a fugitive and a vagabond shalt thou be in the earth.

* Preface to *The Anathemata*, David Jones, Faber, 1952, pp. 20–1.

And Cain said unto the Lord, My punishment is greater than I can bear. . . .

And Cain went out from the presence of the Lord.

(Genesis, IV. vv. 8–13)

The main points of the story are as follows:

(1) The murder is secret, but it is revealed supernaturally.

(2) Its punishment is both divinely ordained and at the same time the natural consequence of the crime: the earth is polluted and will not bear fruit.

(3) The murderer is not killed but suffers an indescribable agony from his doom of exile.

In the Wakefield play, *The Killing of Abel*, the death scene is simple and vigorous:

> CAIN: With cheek-bone e're my hand I stay
> I shall have torn thy life away
> So lie down there and take thy rest,
> So braying curs are chastised best.
>
> ABEL: Vengeance, vengeance Lord, I cry!
> For I am slain and not guilty.
>
> CAIN: Yea lie thou there, wretch, lie there, lie.*

The highly polished stanzas of the Anglo-Norman *Mistère du Viel Testament*† express the fundamental emotions of the characters with more literary sophistication but not more directly.

> Cayn
> Le vella mort;
> Il en est fait!
> Soit droit ou tort,
> Le vela (sic) mort;
> Point de resort
> N'a en ce fait,

---

* *The Wakefield Mystery Plays*, ed. M. Rose, Evans, 1961, p. 24.
† Paris, Firmin Didot, 1878.

Le vela mort;
Il en est fait.
La Voix du Sang qui crie a Dieu, et ne la voit on
point.
Justice, Justice divine,
Venez le sang juste venger,
Que voyez ainsi le danger!
Abel est mort, mys a ruyne.
Justice
Il est force que je m'encline
A escouter ce messager.
La Voix
Justice, Justice divine,
Venez le sang juste venger!*

Sometimes the note of tragedy is changed to one of pawky humour:

GOD: Cain, Cain!

CAIN: Who is that that calls me?
Look I am here, may thou not see?

GOD: Where is thy brother Abel?

CAIN: Why ask of me? I think in hell,
I trust in hell he be—
As any there might see—
Or somewhere fallen a-sleeping;
When was he in my keeping?

GOD: Cain, Cain, thou art caught in a fierce flood;
The voice of thy brother's blood
That thou hast slain in such false wise,
From earth to heaven vengeance cries.
And for thou hast brought thy brother down,
Under the flood of my fury drown.

CAIN: Yea, deal out curses, I will none,
Or give them back when thou hast done.†

---

* Op. cit., pp. 2737–45 and 2752–9.
† *The Wakefield Mystery Plays*, p. 25.

B

Perhaps the Chester version catches more of the tragedy of Cain's fate, a tragedy so clear in later secular plays.

Cayne Lamentat

(84)

> Out! out! alas! alas!
> I am damned without grace,
> Therefore I will from place to place,
> And loke where is the best.
>
> Well I wot and witter lye,
> into what place that come I,
> each man will loth my company;
> so shall I never have rest.

(85)

> Foule hep is me befall:
> wheither I be in howse or hall,
> cursed Cayne men will me call,
> from sorrow may non me save.*

From this starting point the dramatisation of violent death followed by retribution runs through Elizabethan and Jacobean tragedy, and the trail can be picked up again in the very different climate of opinion which conditions the creative arts today. In both periods the greatest plays pay as much attention to the doom of Cain, a punishment greater than he could bear, as to his original act, and this is superbly illustrated in the greatest of all murder plays—*Macbeth*, whose parallels with the Biblical prototype are of particular interest. In each story two contrasted types face each other: the Christ figures of Duncan and Abel are opposed to the Satanic ones of Macbeth and Cain—destroyers, ready to strike whoever stands in their path, whether with the jawbones of an ass or a Renaissance dagger.

And Abel was a keeper of sheep . . . And it came to pass when

* *The Chester Plays*, ii: 'The Creation', E.E.T.S. Extra Series LXII, ll. 665–76.

they were in the field that Cain rose up against Abel his brother and slew him.

> He's here in double trust;
> First as I am his kinsman . . .
> Besides, this Duncan
> Hath born his Faculties so meek . . .   (I. 7.)

And [the Lord] said, What hast thou done? the voice of thy brother's blood crieth unto me from the ground.

> It will have blood, they say!
> Blood will have Blood.   (III. 4.)

Macbeth, however, is primarily concerned with the self-destruction which his own deed at last brings upon the murderer himself, and it is here that Biblical parallels are of the greatest interest.

And behold thou hast driven me out from the face of the ground and from thy face shall I be hid and whosoever findeth me shall slay me.

> To be thus, is nothing, but to be safely thus! . . .   (III, 1.)

> There's not a one of them but in his house
> I keep a Servant fee'd.   (III. 4.)

And Cain went out from the presence of the Lord.

> I 'gin to be aweary of the Sun,
> And wish the estate o' the world were now undone.   (v. 5.)

> From this instant,
> There's nothing serious in Mortality . . .   (II. 3.)

> Life's but a walking Shadow, . . .

> It is a Tale
> Told by an Idiot, full of sound and fury
> Signifying nothing.   (v. 5.)

Macbeth has indeed gone out from the presence of God.

In the Christian society evil can and must be considered as part of the divine plan, and specifically the suffering which is punishment for sin must be accepted as divine in origin.

The evil which consists in the defect of action is always caused
by the defect of the agent. But in God there is no defect . . .
Nevertheless the order of justice belongs to the order of the universe;
and this requires that penalty should be dealt out to sinners. And
so God is the author of the evil which is penalty but not of the evil
which is fault. *

The subtleties of the schoolmen have ceased to express the
dominant morality of society, but many people continue to
admit responsibility for 'the defect of the agent' and are
therefore driven also to commit 'the evil which is penalty'.
This attitude is reflected with unusual clarity in *Rosmersholm*.† In this play Beata, the dead wife, haunting the minds
of both Rebecca and John, calls out for vengeance as clearly as
the blood of Abel or the ghost who cried 'like an oyster wife
"Hamlet revenge" ', and her voice is obeyed.

REBECCA: Where I have sinned it is right that I should expiate . . .
ROSMER: . . . There is no judge over us. And therefore we must
see to it that we judge ourselves.

The housekeeper sees them throw themselves into the river
where Beata also was drowned.

Ah! Over the bridge–both of them! Out into the mill-race. Help!
Help! . . . No. No help here. The dead mistress has taken them. ‡

Whether the writer is aware of it or not, such symbolic significance of character and circumstance is due to the ways of
thought reflected in the following analysis of scriptural exegesis in the Middle Ages.

This familiar procession of patriarchs and prophets, the Saviour

* Thomas Aquinas, *Summa Theologiae*, I, qu. 49., art. 2, trans. Fathers
of the English Dominican Province, Burns, Oates and Washbourne, 1932.
† H. Ibsen, trans. Una Ellis-Fermor (in *The Master Builder and Other
Plays*), Penguin Books, 1958, p. 188b.
‡ Op. cit., pp. 117 and 119.

and his Apostles, was the literal, historical sense, which the scholar shared with the laity. Another procession walked beside it, more sharply outlined, darker or brighter. Here were the types of the spiritual interpretation, the Church and the Synagogue, virtues and vices, the Old Testament's foreshadowing of the New. The layman was just able to perceive them. He saw them in windows and on the walls of churches; he heard hints of them in sermons . . . the spiritual interpretation will penetrate language, thought, politics and finally everyday life.*

A return to a drama of symbols rather than characters became marked in the somewhat ephemeral expressionist plays of the 1920's. Hugo von Hofmansthal in an introduction to Brecht's *Baal* wrote in 1926:

Our time is unredeemed; and do you know what it wants to be redeemed from? . . . the individual . . . Our age groans too heavily under the weight of this child of the sixteenth century that the nineteenth fed to enormous size . . . Individuality is an arabesque we have discarded . . .†

Martin Esslin reports an entertaining comment on the new trend made by Brecht himself in connection with the censorship of his film *Kuhle Wampe* in 1932.

The censor criticised the film because it neglected the individual features of the characters and showed them . . . as generalised types. The young worker who committed suicide thus appeared not as an individual instance but as the representative of all young workers who were denied the right to live. 'No, gentlemen', he exclaimed, 'you have not acted as artists. You were not concerned in showing a tragic individual case' . . . Brecht, with his usual cynicism came to the rescue: 'I rose . . . I stuck strictly to the untruth. I quoted the individual features we had given our unemployed: for example that he had put away his wristwatch before

* B. Smalley, *The Study of the Bible in the Middle Ages*, Clarendon Press, 1941, pp. 24–5.
† Quoted by Martin Esslin, *Bertolt Brecht*, Eyre & Spottiswoode, 1959, p. 29.

jumping out of the window' . . . The film was passed with a few minor cuts. Brecht notes: 'Leaving the building we did not conceal our high opinion of the censor. He had penetrated the essence of our artistic intuitions with far greater sagacity than our most benevolent critics!' *

In the new theatre of types it is not strange to find that the myths which our forebears used serve us as well. A play as different from *Rosmersholm* as *Cross-Purpose* by Albert Camus also harks back to the story of Cain. On the morning after the murder of her son the mother says:

No doubt this is my punishment, and for all murderers a time comes when, like me, they are dried up within, sterile, with nothing left to live for. That's why society gets rid of them. They're good for nothing. . . . I have lost my freedom and my hell has begun. . . . It's no more than the pain of feeling love rekindle in my heart; and yet it's too much for me. I know that this pain too doesn't make sense. . . . But then this world we live in doesn't make sense, and I have a right to judge it, since I've tested all it has to offer, from creation to destruction.†

Such loss of the power to love is one of the most subtle and terrible of all the interpretations of Cain's punishment. It is significant that the dramatic character, though certainly not the author, dismisses it as irrelevant in an irrational universe.

In Harold Pinter's *The Dumb Waiter* one of the two thugs is haunted by the memory of the bloodshed following the murder of a girl.

GUS: What a mess. Honest, I can't remember a mess like that one. They don't seem to hold together like men, women. A looser texture like. Didn't she spread, eh? She didn't half spread. Kaw!

In this play the divine voice comes down the speaking tube of

---

* Op. cit., p. 48.

† *Caligula and Cross-Purpose*, trans. Stuart Gilbert, Hamish Hamilton, 1947, pp. 154–5.

the dumb-waiter, and it is not clear whether Gus is to be liquidated because he committed murder or because he regretted having committed it. What is clear, however, is that to this author the means of retribution can only be human. The end of the play shows two Cains facing each other at the moment of truth, after one killing has already been committed. They then become potentially Cain and Abel and the decision to shoot or to refrain from shooting is entirely Ben's. If he refuses to kill there is no other means of punishment suggested, and if he kills he re-enacts his role of destroyer. His decision is left open:

(The whistle in the speaking-tube blows. He (Ben) takes the whistle out and puts the tube to his ear. He listens . . .)

BEN: Understood. Repeat. He has arrived and will be coming in straight away. The normal method to be employed. Understood . . . Sure we're ready . . . Right . . .

(The door right opens sharply. Ben turns his revolver levelled at the door. Gus stumbles in. He is stripped of his jacket, waistcoat, tie, holster and revolver. He stops, body stooping, his arms at his sides. He raises his head and looks at Ben. A long silence. They stare at each other.)*

In Ionesco's *The Lesson*† the act of killing is accepted as the inevitable concomitant of the urge to power in an amoral world. His desire of aggression drives the Professor to numb and dominate his pupil. He is unsatisfied until he has first raped and then killed her. 'Abel' lies crucified across a wooden chair, but there is neither hope nor fear that her blood will cry for vengeance or that, if it did, it would be heard. This destruction will indeed be repeated indefinitely. The girl is the fourteenth victim of the day; her successor knocks at the door as the play finishes, and the woman who knows enough to condemn what is going on, hurries to let her in. In *The Killer*

* *The Birthday Party and Other Plays*, Methuen, 1960, pp. 140 and 158–9.
† *Plays*, I, John Calder, 1958.

Cain and Abel again confront each other, and again the issue is both inevitable and uncondemned. Within the individual as within society the urge to destroy is stronger than the urge to create, and the dance of death woven by the killer around his would-be destroyer is danced, it would appear, within the mind of Everyman. No human avenger can therefore end the conflict, and no divine power interferes to punish or prevent it.

BÉRENGER (*to the Killer*) You kill without reason . . . and I beg you, without reason I implore you, yes, please *stop*. . . There's no reason why you should, naturally, but please stop, just because there's *no reason* to kill or not to kill . . .

(*The Killer chuckles softly; very softly he takes from his pocket a knife with a large shining blade and plays with it.*)

You filthy dirty moronic imbecile! You're ugly as a monkey! Fierce as a tiger, stupid as a mule . . . I'm on my knees, yes . . . but it's not to beg for mercy . . . It's to take better aim . . .

(*Bérenger aims without firing at the Killer . . . whose knife is raised and who is chuckling and quite motionless. Bérenger slowly lowers his two old-fashioned pistols . . . and then, on his knees with his head down and his arms hanging at his side, he stammers:*)

Oh God! There's nothing we can do. What can we do . . . What can we do . . .

(*While the Killer draws nearer, still chuckling, but very very softly.*)*

Here Cain and Abel are once more face to face, and Abel is helpless, a pre-destined victim, for Cain is a part of himself and a part against whom he has no effective weapon. His arguments are derisory, his pistols out of date. But the knife is both as old as mankind and as new; the desire to destroy precedes reason and transcends it; Abel, in the irrational society, is doomed.

In Bertolt Brecht's *Mother Courage*† the two brothers appear drawing the canteen wagon which is both the family's source of being and its means of livelihood. In Brecht's mytho-

* *Plays*, III, John Calder, 1960, pp. 107–9.
† Methuen *Plays*, vol. II, Methuen, 1962.

logy the brothers do not, as individuals, destroy each other: it is society which destroys them both—Eiliff, the natural aggressor, is executed in peace-time for the violence which made him a hero during the war, and 'Swiss Cheese', gentle and loyal, the pre-destined victim, dies in defence of the family which denies him. Brecht goes out of his way to emphasise his Christian prototype, for when the boy is led away to torture and martyrdom and his mother and sister wait, washing up the canteen knives and glasses, the lapsed chaplain sings the ballad of *The Passion of Jesus*.

> Each upon his cross two thieves
> Mocked him like the others.
> And the bright sun crept away
> Not to see such doings. . . .
> Nine: Lord Jesus cried aloud
> That he was forsaken! . . .
> Then the Lord gave up the ghost
> And the earth did tremble. (p. 34)

His mother could still save her son if she would pay all she has to bribe the soldiers, but this she will not do.

MOTHER COURAGE: Don't break the glasses, they're not ours. Watch what you're doing, you're cutting yourself. Swiss Cheese will be back, I'll give two hundred, if it's necessary. You'll get your brother back. . . . You should rub them dry, I said.

(They clean the knives in silence. Suddenly Katrin runs sobbing behind the wagon . . . In the distance a roll of drums . . . Mother Courage remains seated. It grows dark. It gets light again. Mother Courage has not moved.)

'The bright sun crept away not to see such doings', but the two-fold denial is still to be made. The soldiers bring in the body thinking to shock the old woman into recognition of the dead man. A friend brings the warning:

YVETTE: You'd better not know him or we're in for it. And I'd

better tell you straight, they're just behind me. Shall I keep
Katrin away ? . . Does she know? Maybe she never heard the
drums or didn't understand.

MOTHER COURAGE: She knows. Bring her.

(*Yvette brings Katrin, who walks over to her mother and stands by
her. Mother Courage takes her hand. Two men come in with a
stretcher; there is a sheet on it, and something underneath. . . .*)

SERGEANT: Here's a man we don't know the name of. But he has
to be registered to keep the records straight. He bought a meal
from you. Look at him, see if you know him. (*He pulls back the
sheet.*) Do you know him? (*Mother Courage shakes her head.*)
What? You never saw him before he took that meal? (*Mother
Courage shakes her head.*) Lift him up. Throw him in the carrion
pit. He has no one that knows him. (pp. 39–40)

Brecht does not allow the innocent blood to cry for vengeance
nor the cock to crow to mark its betrayal any more than he
allows a ram to be caught in a thicket and used as a vicarious
sacrifice. The deaths of all her children do not save Mother
Courage. She is left to pull her rotting wagon by herself along
her lonely path because she failed to understand the nature of
the society in which she lived. In Brecht's dramatic cosmos an
impersonal 'justice' from which there can be no appeal condemns alike all those who fail to learn the lessons of the social
facts which are open to their observation.

ii. THE BLOOD THAT CRIED FROM THE GROUND

The earth hath not a hole to hide this deed
Murder as hating what himself hath done
Doth lay it open to urge on revenge.
(*King John*, IV. iii.)

When English drama moved from the use of religious to
that of secular material, the climate of opinion was still such
that faith in divine retribution for sin was an unchallenged
axiom; the presentation of such retribution in the theatre
represented no sentimental fantasy or cynical concession to

commercial advantages but was a true reflection of an accepted social 'ethos', traceable in all the current forms of literature. When, for example, Holinshed tells of the murder of the two little princes in the Tower, he alludes directly to the prototype of Cain and Abel: 'The blood of which seelie and little babes dailie crie to God from the earth for vengeance'.*

Sir Walter Raleigh in the Preface to his *History of the World*, clothes this faith in all the magnificence of his splendid prose. He insists on the grim reality of punishment for sin, for 'the blood that is unjustly shed is not again gathered up from the ground by repentance', 'the secret and unsearchable judgment of God' can ensure that 'buildings of which the mortar had been tempered with innocent blood', will fall, if not on the man who raised them, then on his children and grandchildren.

The judgements of God are for ever unchangeable; neither is he wearied by the long process of time, and wont to give his blessing in one age, to that which he hath cursed in another. . . . Yet when we once come in sight of the Port of Death, to which all winds drive us; and when by letting fall that fatal anchor, which can never be weighed again, the Navigation of this life takes end: then it is I say, that our own cogitations (those sad and severe cogitations, formerly beaten from us by our Health and Felicity) return again, and pay us to the uttermost for all the pleasing passages of our lives past. It is then that we cry out to God for mercy; then, when ourselves can no longer exercise cruelty to others: and it is only then that we are strucken through the soul with this terrible sentence, That God will not be mocked . . . But of this composition are all the devout lovers of the world, that they fear all that is dureless and ridiculous; they fear the plots and practices of their opposites, and their very whisperings; they fear the opinions of men which beat but upon shadows: . . . yea, they dive under water, like ducks, at every pebble stone that is but thrown towards them by a powerful hand; and on the contrary, they show an obstinate and giantlike valour, against the terrible judgements of the All-powerful God.†

* Holinshed's *Chronicles*, vol. III, London, 1808, p. 407.
† Folio Edition. Spelling modernised by author. Pages A3, B3, C4, D.

On this theme even the popular melodramas achieve some measure of dignity. A genuine sense of urgency may be caught in the following lines from *A Warning to Fair Women,** a play which has, for the most part, no poetic quality.

BROWNE: Let us study now
How we may solve it, and conceal the fact.

ANNE: Mountains will not suffice to cover it;
  Cymmerian darkness cannot shadow it;
  Nor any pollicie wit hath in store
  Cloak it so cunningly, but at the last
  If nothing else, yet will the very stones
  That lie within the streetes cry out for vengeance,
  And point at us to be the murderers.   (II. ll. 762–8.)

A late example, of interest because it also is from popular literature and illustrates the persistence in men's minds of the original story, is a broadside ballad† concerning the murder of Sir Thomas Overbury.

> Within this house of Death a dead man lies,
> Whose blood, like Abel's, up for vengeance cries;
> Time hath revealed what to trueth belongs,
> And Justice sword is drawn to right my wrongs.

The broadside is illustrated by the figures of Time and Justice on either side of a tomb on which lies a skeleton.

The certain revelation of secret murder, imaged in the Bible by the blood of Abel crying from the ground, is given various dramatic forms. Some stem from folk-lore and perhaps the most obvious example is the bleeding of the corpse in the presence of the murderer, a symbol of which Shakespeare himself makes use:

* *The School of Shakespeare*, Chatto & Windus, 1878.
† *The Knight's Complaint*, imprinted at London for John White, 1615.

ANNE: (of Henry's corpse, to Richard)
    If thou delightest to view thy heinous deeds,
    Behold this pattern of thy butcheries.
    O gentlemen, see see dead Henry's wounds
    Open their congealed mouths and bleed afresh.
    Blush, blush thou lump of foul deformity,
    For 't is thy presence which exhales this blood
    From cold and empty veins where no blood dwells:
    Thy deed unhuman and unnatural
    Provokes this deluge most unnatural.
                          (*Richard III*, I. ii.)

The superstition is used in a more naturalistic way in *A Warning to Fair Women* when Browne is brought face to face with the dying Beane. Here the voice of a man, believed to be dead, closely relates the symbol of the blood that speaks to that of the ghost who returns.

MAYOR: See if this poor soule know him.

BARNES: It cannot be; these two days' space
    He knew no creature.

BROWNE: Swounds, lives the villaine yet? (aside).
    His very eyes will speake had he no tongue
    And will accuse me.

BARNES: See how his wounds break out afresh in bleeding.

M. JAMES: He stirs himselfe.

MAYOR: He openeth his eyes.

BARNES: See how he looks upon him.

BROWNE I gave him fifteene wounds, (aside)
    Which now be fifteene mouthes that doe accuse me;
    In ev'ry wound there is a bloody tongue,
    Which will all speake, although he hold his peace;
    By a whole jury I shall be accused.

BARNES: John, dost thou heare? Knowest thou this man?

BEANE: Yea, this is he that murdered me and Mr Sanders . . .

BARNES: Sure the revealing of this murther's strange.

M. JAMES: It is so, sir, but in the case of blood,
   God's justice hath bin still miraculous.   (II. ll. 1030–61.)

The device of a voice speaking from a body believed to be dead
is used also by Shakespeare in *Othello*, but when Desdemona
speaks from her bed of death it is not to curse but to forgive:

> EMILIA: Oh who hath done this deed?
>
> DESDEMONA: Nobody; I myself, farewell;
>   Commend me to my kind Lord: oh farewell. (V. 2.)

It is a measure of Othello's fall from grace that the force of
the contrast between what he must have expected to hear
when she speaks and what he actually does hear still does not
suffice to shock him into the realisation of her innocence.

The impossibility of removing the stain of innocent blood
was a commonplace before Macbeth could cry:

> Will all great Neptune's Ocean wash this blood
> Clean from my Hand?

or Lady Macbeth learned that her hands could 'ne'er be clean',
and when she moans 'Here's the smell of blood still' her words
transcend any expression of individual guilt. For ordinary
people the dumb eloquence of the blood that will not out long
remained charged with associations of divine vengeance on the
murder of Abel. Such a contemporary figure as the goldsmith,
John Brewen, whose story is told by Thomas Kyd, is introduced thus:

How hatefull a thing the sinne of murder hath beene before the
sight of the eternall God, the holy Scriptures doe manifest; yet from
the beginning we may evidently see how busie the divell hath beene
to provoke men thereunto, in so much that when there was [sic] but
two brethren living in the world, the onelye sonnes of the first man,
Adam, hee provoked the one most unnaturally to murther the
other. And albeit there was none in the world to accuse Caine for
so fowle a fact, so that in his owne conceit hee might have walked

securely and without blame, yet the blood of the just Abel cried
most shrill in the eares of the righteous God for vengeance and
revinge on the murderer. The Lord therefore ordayned a Lawe that
the cruel and unjust blood-sheader [sic] should have his blood justly
shed again.*

That such a grim superstition could occasionally be used
more lightly is shown in a delicately frivolous little love lyric
by William Strode.†

> What mystery was this that I should find
> My blood in kissing you to stay behind? . . .
> If at the presence of a murderer
> The wounds will bleede and tell the cause is there,
> A touch will doe much more, and this my heart,
> When secretly it felt the killing darte
> Shew'd it in blood: which yet doth more complayne
> Because I cannot so be touched againe;
> Here I could spill it all: thus I can free
> Mine enemy from blood, though slayne I be:
> But slayne I cannot bee, nor meete with ill,
> Since but by you I have no blood to spill.

The divine control of apparent chance was seen with particular clarity in those cases where the wicked man himself
walked unwittingly into the trap he had laid for others. A
favourite example was the Bible story of Haman, told in the
book of Esther, where Haman is hanged on the gallows he has
set up for Mordecai. The story was dramatised at least twice.

> ARBONA: There is in the house of this traitor Aman,
> A pair of gallows of fifty cubits high;
> Upon them he had thought, either now or then
> To have caused Mardocheus to die.

* From *The Works of Thomas Kyd*, ed. F. S. Boas, Oxford, 1902: 'The
Murder of John Brewen . . . who was poisoned of his owne wife in eating a
measse of sugarsops,' 1592.

† B.M.M.S. Hav. 6917, and *Poetical Works of William Strode*, ed.
Dobell, published by the editor 1907.

ASSUERUS: Lead him hence, and upon them, by and by,
See that ye hang him, and so stop his breath.
(*Godly Queen Hester*, p. 282.)*

The author of *The Atheist's Tragedy*† writes with some
sensitiveness about the relations of justice and vengeance in
the ordered universe, although at the end of his play he
invokes the folk belief that the murderer will become his own
executioner in a manner as crude as that of the popular drama
of half a century earlier. D'Amville mocks Charlement and
prides himself on his own lack of superstition, but before his
death he is to learn differently; he grows mad and in the fury
of his distraction he leaps on to the scaffold on which Charlement is awaiting execution.

D'AMVILLE: I ha' the trick on't, nephew. You shall see
How easily I can put you out of pain.—Oh.

(*As he raises up the axe he strikes out his own
brains, and staggers off the scaffold.*)

EXECUTIONER: In lifting up the axe,
I think he knocked his brains out.

In spite of the almost comic banality of the last line we are
reminded of another nephew listening to words spoken of
another murderous and usurping Uncle:

It is a poison tempered by himself.

The Atheist's Tragedy shows 'poetic justice', stark and incredible because unveiled by pattern or poetry, but even in
Hamlet a large proportion of the main events which carry
forward the action of the play appear as merely chance, the
work of Fortune in her most casual, most random capacity.‡
Such coincidences, however, do in fact ensure that the en-

* *Six Anonymous Plays* (Second Series), ed. J. S. Farmer, Early English
Dramatists, 1906.

† Webster and Tourneur, ed. J. A. Symonds, Mermaid Series, Benn,
1948.

‡ John Holloway, *The Story of the Night*, pp. 34–6 London, 1961.

2. Justice and Innocence: a tapestry after Bronzino.
By Giovanni Rost, c. 1548.

gineer is hoist with his own petard. 'I am a woodcock caught in mine own springe', says Laertes; Guildenstern and Rosencrantz die by the warrant they were carrying to ensure another's death; Claudius' poisoned chalice is at last presented to his own lips, as was Macbeth's to his. The pattern is simple, and it is powerful because of its simplicity.

The passage of *Two Lamentable Tragedies** in which the discovery of Beech's mutilated corpse is described by its finder, while the porter carrying the body stands beside him, is a parallel case, and its freshness merits quotation.

> Walking betime by Paris-garden ditch,
> Hauing my Water-Spaniell by my side,
> When we approach'd vnto that haplesse place
> Where this same trunke lay drowned in a ditch,
> My Spaniell gan to sent, to barke, to plunge
> Into the water, and came foorth againe,
> And fawn'd on me, as if a man should say,
> Helpe out a man that heere lyes murthered.
> At first I tooke delight to see the dog,
> Thinking in vaine some game did there lye hid
> Amongst the Nettles growing nerre the banke:
> But when no game, nor anything appear'd,
> That might produce the Spaniell to this sport,
> I gan to rate and beate the harmlesse Cur, ...
> But still he plung'd, he diu'd, he barkt, he ran
> Still to my side, as if it were for helpe.
> I seeing this, did make the ditch be dragd,
> Where then was found this body as you see.

If men will only wait justice will certainly be achieved.

> Wherefore if we our follies would refrain
> Time would redress all wrongs, we void of pain.
> (*Mirror for Magistrates*, Jack Cade, ll. 1601–2.)

* *Two Lamentable Tragedies: The one, of the murther of Maister Beech á Chaundler in Thomas-Streete, and his boye*, done by Thomas Merry . . . 1601 in *A Collection of Old English Plays*, ed. A. H. Bullen, 1882–9, vol. 4, p. 66.

c

Quince challenges his auditors to 'wonder on till time makes all things plain,' *Midsummer Night's Dream*, v and a later play is more pretentious, though not more succinct. *The Whore of Babylon** opens with a dumb show concerning Time and his daughter Truth, in which at length these figures, who appear at first in 'sad habiliments' return to prefigure the final triumph of virtue.

Time being shifted into light colours, his properties likewise altered into silver and Truth crowned (being clothed in a robe spotted with stars) . . . and pulling the veils from the councillors' eyes, they wondering a while and seeming astonished at her bright-ness, at length embrace Truth and Time and depart with them. (p. 500)

The last lines of the first English secular tragedy had made the same assertion:

> Of justice yet must God in fine† restore
> This noble crown unto the lawful heirs:
> For right will always live and rise at length,
> But wrong can never take deep root to last.
> (*Gorboduc*, v. 2.)‡

A still more powerful image of the workings of divine justice was found in the fact that a man's guilt may be the cause of his own punishment. A simple example is to be found in *Arden of Feversham*, where Alice and the maid in their confusion fail to destroy the most obvious evidence of their guilt, so that the blood-stained cloth and knife remain to betray them as a result of their own failure to throw them down the well. In *Two Lamentable Tragedies* equally realistic detail is more explicitly related to spiritual distress. Merrie and his sister are in their kitchen, and Beech's corpse is hidden under the firewood.

---

* Dekker, *Dramatic Works*, Vol. II, ed. F. Bowers, Cambridge, 1955.
† i.e. 'at last'.
‡ *Minor Elizabethan Drama*, Everyman Library 491, Dent, 1958.

MERRY: Sister, now all my golde-expected hopes
  Of future good, is plainely vanished,
  And in her stead grim visadged dispaire,
  Hath tane possession of my guiltie heart, . . .

RACHELL: Ah, do not so disconsolate your selfe,
  Nor adde new streames of sorrow to your griefe, . . .
  Whither would you conuey this lumpe of dust
  Vntimely murthered by your lucklesse hand? . . .

MERRY: For if we keepe it longer in the house,
  The sauour will be smelt throughout the streete,
  Which will betray vs to destruction.
  Oh what a horror brings this beastlinesse.

RACHELL: Those little stickes, do hide the murthred course,
  But stickes, nor ought besides, can hide the sinne: . . .

MERRY: Look euerywhere, can you discerne him now?

RACHELL: Not with mine eye, but with my heart I can.

The Elizabethans were much concerned with the workings of the guilty mind. In 1579, Thomas Twyne in his translation of Petrarch's *De Remedeis Utruisque Fortuna* wrote: 'There is no worse war than this, no not civile warre: For that is between factions of citizens in the streetes of the cities, but this fought within the mind betweene the parties of the soule.'*

The historian Holinshed foreshadows Shakespeare's play when he analyses the distress of Richard III before the battle of Bosworth.

The fame went, that he had the same night a dreadfull and terrible dreame: for it seemed to him being asleepe, that he did see diverse images like terrible devils, which pulled and mauled him, not suffering him to take anie quiet or rest. The which strange vision not so suddenlie stroke his heart with a sudden feare, but it stuffed his head and troubled his mind with many busie and dreadful imaginations. . . . I think this was no dream, but a punction and pricke of his sinful conscience.†

* Quoted in Farnham, *Medieval Heritage of Elizabethan Tragedy*, Blackwell, 1963, p. 51.   † v. supra, p. 27.

Hamlet, whatever other undertones of meaning the words may convey, was voicing a contemporary commonplace when he declared that 'conscience doth make cowards of us all', and Iachimo experienced in fact what Hamlet only thought about:

> The heaviness and guilt within my bosom,
> Takes off my manhood; I have belied a Lady,
> The Princess of this Country; and the air on't
> Revengingly enfeebles me, or could this Carl,
> A very drudge of Nature's, have subdued me
> In my profession?
>
> <div align="right">(<i>Cymbeline</i>, v. 2.)</div>

In point of fact Iachimo had not been subdued by a carl, but even when he knows who his victor was he continues to admit the source of his weakness:

> I am down again:
> But now my heavy Conscience sinks my knee,
> As then thy force did.
>
> <div align="right">(<i>Cymbeline</i>, v. 5.)</div>

Indeed, 'this was no dreame, but a punction and pricke of his sinfull conscience'.

The steady progress of a guilty man's self-destruction is one of the major themes in *Macbeth*. At the beginning of the play Macbeth could claim to be a 'great and complete man'. He can truly say to his wife:

> I dare do all that may become a man,
> Who dares do more, is none.
>
> (i. 7.)

Lady Macbeth offers a false criterion of manhood—the ability to kill:

> When thou durst do it, then you were a man;
> And to be more than what you were, you would

Be so much more the man. Nor time, nor place
Did then adhere, and yet you would make both;
They have made themselves, and that their fitness now
Does unmake you.*

(I. 7.)

Later Macbeth has adopted his wife's values; he demands of
his assassins that they assess the quality of their manhood by
their willingness to murder their enemy:

> Ay, in the catalogue ye go for men . . .
> Now, if you have a station in the file,
> Not i' the worst rank of Manhood, say it,
> And I will put that Business in your bosoms,
> Whose execution takes your enemy off. . . .

(III. i.)

He still, however, himself retains some title to true manhood,
for his inner horror of himself is reflected in his reactions to
Banquo's ghost. His wife at this time can still ask him:

> Are you a man?

and accuse him of being

> quite unmanned in folly,

while Macbeth defends his fear of the ghost as natural:

> What man dares, I dare,

but when his fear passes he again equates manhood with the
loss of humanity:

> Why so, being gone
> I am a man again.   (III. 4.)

He proceeds to assert this false manhood by going on to plan

* i.e. unman, dehumanise.

the murder of Macduff, who, when he hears of the death of all
his 'pretty chickens and their dam', grows in stature to the full
and true manhood which Macbeth has forfeited. When Malcolm urges him to 'dispute it like a man', he answers:

> I shall do so:
> But I must also feel it as a man.   (IV. i.)

'No mind that's honest' dissents from his decision of vengeance
on the murderer, and he undertakes this deliberately and in
the eye of heaven:

> gentle Heavens,
> Cut short all intermission: Front to Front
> Set thou this Fiend of Scotland, and myself
> Within my sword's length set him, if he scape
> Heaven forgive him too.

MALCOLM: This tune goes manly.   (IV. 1.)

Young Siward, who 'only lived but till he was a man,' proved
his manhood by both recognizing and challenging evil:

MACBETH: My name's Macbeth.

Y. SIWARD: The devil himself could not pronounce a Title
More hateful to mine ear.

MACBETH: No: nor more fearful.

Y. SIWARD: Thou liest abhorred Tyrant, with my Sword
I'll prove the lie thou speakest.

Because he was no more than a man the challenge cost him his
life:

MACBETH: Thou wast born of woman.   (V. 7.)

'He lived but till he was a man' and yet 'like a man he died'.
When Macduff faces Macbeth he knows he faces a man who
has become a beast: 'Turn Hell-hound, turn.' Certain of victory,

Macbeth stifles his last breath of the remorse which made him
say:

MACBETH: But get thee back, my soul is too much charged
With blood of thine already . . .

In his arrogance he ignores the voice of his own conscience and
attacks the truly 'great and complete man' which Macduff has
become, only to find in him the instrument of the 'powers
above':

MACBETH: Thou losest labour,
I bear a charmed Life.

MACDUFF: Despair thy Charm,
And let the Angel whom thou still hast served
Tell thee, Macduff was from his Mother's womb
Untimely ripped.   (v. 8.)

Lady Macbeth's destruction is even more obviously self-
imposed than is her husband's. The 'spirits that tend on
mortal thoughts' destroy her as certainly as they enabled her
to destroy Duncan, and she called them up herself. The
muttering, moaning sleepwalker is the pallid ghost of the
flashing creature who earlier bent men to her will as she
chose. She has even lost the power of coherent speech; the
language of her agony in guilt disintegrates to 'Oh, oh, oh.'

iii. A SPANISH TRAGEDY AND THE PERSONAL AVENGER

For I must be their scourge and minister.
(*Hamlet*, III.)

Men are not easily content to leave the righting of wrong to
Truth, the daughter of Time, nor to social institutions which
they know by experience to be fallible. On the contrary among
their most urgent preoccupations is their concern to redress
the disturbed balance of human affairs themselves, according to

such insight into the order of the universe as they possess. It is
a preoccupation ubiquitous in dramatic literature, where both
the private blood-feud with its danger, suspense and violent
climax, and the trial by society with its panoply, pattern and
verbal warfare, offer to the dramatist situations of intrinsically
theatrical quality made ready to his hand.

Thomas Kyd's brilliant contribution to the dramatisation of
personal vengeance was to devise a dramatic convention by
which the killing of the sinner was distanced and stylised into
a ritual, so that it could be accepted as inevitable and righteous.

*A Spanish Tragedy** was probably first performed in the
late 1580's. Its record in the Elizabethan–Jacobean period
shows that it must have both satisfied a need and stimulated a
demand. It was acted in London twenty-three times between
1592–3 and continued to be performed until at least 1615. It
was paid the compliment of parody, and references to it during
this period are innumerable. It was first published in 1592 and
republished nine times before the last edition in 1633.

We must consider here not such obvious dramatic merits as
its characterisation, its swift dialogue and evocative lyric verse
but rather its structure, for it is this which makes a unique
contribution to the dramatisation of sin and justice. Its meticulously constructed plot makes each human action play its
part in fulfilling the will of the gods as this is shown in the
Prologue, where Persephone promises vengeance on Balthazar to the ghost of Andrea, who thus becomes the prototype of all the later spirits who voice the cry of innocent
blood.

ANDREA: Forthwith, Revenge, she rounded thee in th' ear
   And bade thee lead me through the gates of horn,
   Where dreams have passage in the silent night . . .

REVENGE: . . . know, Andrea, that thou art arriv'd
   Where thou shalt see the author of thy death, [i.e. Balthazar]
   Depriv'd of life by Bel-Imperia:
   Here sit we down to see the mystery.†

(I. i. ll. 81–90.)

* Ed. P. Edwards, *Revel Plays*, Methuen, 1959.   † i.e. sacred drama.

Andrea's death is thus important at the beginning of the play, but he is speedily forgotten by the other characters–Bel-Imperia, his mistress, finally seeks vengeance for her new lover Horatio, and Heironymo, the father of Horatio, does so for his son; Lorenzo pursues his dynastic ambitions and Balthazar his passion for Bel-Imperia. By their logical pursuit of their own ends, however, Balthazar dies. Forgotten by the protagonists of the story – and probably by the reader – Andrea is never forgotten by the audience in the theatre, for he is visibly present on the stage during the whole performance. There is no sign that the workings of the pagan gods are here considered to be the activities of evil powers. They answer the cry of innocent blood as inevitably as does the power which ensures the punishment of Macbeth, and the murderer himself opens the way for his undoing, since Lorenzo plans the masque in which he meets his death.

Here, however, the actual author of vengeance is neither chance nor the murderer himself nor the state, but an individual human being acting personally when his attempt to win justice from law or prince has failed,* and he goes about his vengeance in a particular way, a way which Kyd originated as a dramatic device. After a long lapse of time, during which the potential avenger awaits his opportunity protected by a pose of madness until he is sure of the guilt of the murderers, there is offered, apparently by chance, an opportunity for achieving the vengeance which has been so long delayed. This chance is the presentation of a play in which Bel-Imperia, Lorenzo, Balthazar and Heironymo himself, act before the King. This play provides an exact parallel to the events of the characters' real lives, and Heironymo is cast to enact the murder of Lorenzo, and Bel-Imperia that of Balthazar, before she takes her own life. Instead of tragedy reflecting a 'real' death in mime, this tragedy *is* in itself the 'real' death of its characters, and its killings appear as ritual sacrifices, carried out with formal moves and formal language by characters specially

* V. Act III. 4.

robed for their parts, embodying before a congregation a
sacred symbol of the ways of God. When the ritual is completed its high priest returns to the everyday world at the
moment when he draws the curtain to reveal the body of his
dead son and explains the mystery within a 'mystery'. After
pointing to the three dead bodies, he says:

> Behold the reason urging me to this.
>
> (*Shows his dead son.*)
>
> See here my show, look on my spectacle:
> Here lay my hope, and here my hope hath end;
> Here lay my heart, and here my heart was slain; . . .
> Speak, Portuguese, whose loss resembles mine:
> If thou canst weep upon thy Balthazar,
> 'Tis like I wail'd for my Horatio.
> And you, my Lord, whose reconciled son
> March'd in a net, and thought himself unseen,
> And rated me for brainsick lunacy,
> With 'God amend that mad Heironymo!'—
> How can you brook our play's catastrophe?
>
> (IV. 4, ll. 88–121.)

When his purpose has thus been attained he kills himself. The
touches of realism, such as Lorenzo's quoted words, serve to
give body to an essentially symbolic situation in which two
lives are paid for by two lives, and the two who exact payment,
themselves pay the same penalty, so that no further need for
vengeance remains.

Thus the earth, which received the blood of the innocent,
sends out, through the ghost of Andrea rising from beneath it,
a voice crying for vengeance, and the punishment of the
murderer is removed from the naturalism of state action,
gang warfare, secret cunning or hand to hand fighting. It
takes place *as a ritual*, an exact balancing of accounts not by
involved and therefore fallible individuals but by disguised
figures working through the formalities of stylised movement
and presenting, as in a mirror, a reflection which makes clear

the absolute significance of particular events. In this way the punishment of 'Cain', though by human hands, is shown as fulfilling the divine purpose, and this interpretation, as Miss Gardner first demonstrated,* is enforced by the fact that the justified avenger has only to wait for the moment in which the sinner himself prepares the trap into which he falls. Thus the dramatic pattern itself demonstrates the contemporary faith that the disturbed balance of the ordered universe will inevitably be restored.

This formalisation of vengeance is a social as well as a dramatic device. When the judge, already remote and elevated, already made a symbolic figure by his robes and wig, is to deliver sentence of death, he still further de-personalises himself by putting on a black cap before he becomes the mouthpiece, who can say: 'I, now the voice of the recorded law' or 'It is the Law, not I, condemn your brother...be content.' (*Measure for Measure*, II. 2.) But for this 'alienation' perhaps no individual in a stable society could pronounce a sentence of death, nor any such society bear to hear it.

However great may be the sense of ritual and necessity, however remote from everyday affairs the taking of a life may be made, there remains the crucial difficulty for a Christian audience that God has expressly forbidden human vengeance. Heironymo, who does in fact undertake it, himself quotes the words of Romans: 'Vengeance is mine; I will repay,' saith the Lord.

HEIRONYMO: *Vindicta Mihi*:
    Ay, heaven will be revenged of every ill,
    Nor will they suffer murder unrepaid:
    Then stay, Heironymo, attend their will,
    For mortal men may not appoint their time.
                                        (III. xiii. ll. 1–5.)

In Kyd's design Heironymo does attend the will of heaven, for it is heaven which appoints a time by allowing the

* *The Business of Criticism*, Oxford, 1959, pp. 37 ff.

murderer himself to offer Heironymo the opportunity of vengeance. It appears certain moreover that the audience's sympathy is demanded for the avenger. Such a feeling is steadily built up from the moment of Heironymo's entry in his nightshirt, carrying his drawn sword and torch and seeking the source of the cry for help which had awoken him. The discovery of the body followed by its recognition is stagecraft of the first order and powerfully demands identification of the audience with the horrified father:

> What outcries pluck me from my naked bed? . . .
> Who calls Heironymo? Speak, here I am.
> I did not slumber, therefore 'twas no dream,
> No, no, it was some woman cried for help, . . .
> But stay, what murd'rous spectacle is this?
> A man hanged up and all the murderers gone,
> And in my bower, to lay the guilt on me: . . .
>
> (*He cuts him down.*)
>
> Those garments that he wears I oft have seen—
> Alas, it is Horatio my sweet son! . . .
> O speak, if any spark of life remain;
> I am thy father. (II. 5. ll. 1–18.)

There follows the touching scene between Heironymo and that other old and bereaved father—*son semblable, son frère*—who in his obsession he takes to be Horatio speaking of his own death:

HEIRONYMO: And art thou come, Horatio, from the depth
To ask for justice in this upper earth? . . .

SENEX: Alas my lord, whence springs this troubled speech . . .
I am a grieved man, and not a ghost,
That came for justice for my murder'd son.

HEIRONYMO: Ay, now I know thee, now thou nam'st thy son,
Thou art the lively image of my grief:
Within thy face my sorrows I may see. . . .
Come in old man . . .
Lean on my arm. (III. xiii. ll. 133–171.)

We are thus left with the paradox of the righteous and theatrically sympathetic character who has transgressed divine law in the service of divine law. As he has killed the punishment he merits is death, yet as a hero fulfilling a divinely enjoined task he must not become the next sacrifice in a vendetta which would degrade him to the level of his victim. The only courses open to the dramatist and acceptable to an 'involved' audience are either to allow the hero a justified suicide or to arrange that he dies in the performance of his duty. Suicide, which was under a strong religious ban, could not be a permanently satisfactory device, though it was apparently accepted in Heironymo's case. The other method is that used at the end of *Hamlet*. It must be recognised that in its structure Shakespeare's *Hamlet*—like the Ur-Hamlet, probably by Kyd, which preceded it—is a consistent reproduction of the prototype of divinely ordained vengeance established in *A Spanish Tragedy*. It 'is not a drama of weakness but of duty and self-denial'.*
The punishment of a secret bloodshed is as much the unquestioned duty of Hamlet as it is of Heironymo and Titus Andronicus before him or Macduff and Malcolm after him. He is called to his revenge by a spirit whose 'bona fides' are proved by knowledge of the hidden truth, and he delays only until he can identify his enemy with certainty and then strike with reasonable hope of success. His opportunity to do so is given by his enemy, 'working in blindness to his own defeat'. When Hamlet finally takes action there is not so much of ritual remoteness as at the climax of *A Spanish Tragedy*, but the scene is highly patterned. The arrangement of the figures is formal, and the duel—as a brother's wager—was ostensibly as much a mimic killing as the murders in Heironymo's play purported to be. But while this is true and important, it applies only to the death of Laertes, not to that of Claudius which occurs when the ritual of the duel is over and is conducted with extreme brutality and violence. This perhaps is the reason that, as Hamlet is presented to us as truly the

* Boris Pasternak – quoted H. Levin, *The Question of Hamlet*, Oxford, 1959, p. 85.

justicer of God taking advantage of the God-given occasion which the murderer unwittingly prepares, our proper sympathy for him is re-inforced in his death, first by the natural love and loyalty shown between him and Horatio, and secondly by the touching, and, as Bradley pointed out, unusually religious tone of Horatio's farewell.

> Goodnight sweet Prince
> And flights of Angels wing thee to thy rest.

After *Hamlet* Shakespeare had still to write other plays concerning revenge, notably *Macbeth*, in which vengeance is not so much a personal act as an inevitable process, and *Othello*, in which the search for justice becomes a ghastly parody of itself. Shakespeare of course transcends Kyd's old convention, but curious vestigial traces of it remain. No ghost incites Othello, only Iago a true 'Cain', seeking the destruction of goodness which makes him ugly in his own eyes. There is no long pause while the 'Scourge and Minister' waits, hidden in disguise or madness, until truth is made plain and the ordered universe presents him with a god-given opportunity to do the work of God, only a single night of anguish in which vision is clouded by passion and the truth not perceived.

Othello should have known his enterprise was beyond human fulfilment and his failure certain,

> . . . for what other thing can be expected when a man is plaintiff, witness, judge and executioner all himself; but that the action should be rashly commenced, the vileness corrupt, the judgment partial and the execution both sudden and violent.*

He is purposing crude vengeance, yet before undertaking his self-imposed task, Othello solemnly assumes the role of the avenger, of the sacrificing priest he thinks he is. He de-personalises himself in his function, as the judge must always do, and Iago performs a grotesque parody of his act.

* De la Primaudaye, the French academic, London, 1586.

OTHELLO: Look here Iago,
  All my fond love thus do I blow to Heaven. 'Tis gone.
  Arise black vengeance, from the hollow hell,
  Yield up (O Love) thy crown and hearted throne
  To tyrannous hate . . . . .
               Now by yond Marble Heaven,
  In the due reverence of a Sacred vow,
  I here engage my words.

IAGO: Do not rise yet:
  Witness you ever burning Lights above,
  You elements, that clip us round about,
  Witness that here Iago doth give up
  The execution of his wit, hands, heart,
  To wronged Othello's service.   (III. iii.)

Professor Heilman in his detailed study of *Othello** interprets this scene thus:

> In his tragic failure to find the best form of action—to hear the transcendental imperative against vengeance (and thus incidentally to have time to learn the truth that could enable him to execute justice) . . . he at least tries to avoid the extreme formlessness of uninhibited private action. In life as in art the form of an action may reveal the content . . . Order is still imaginable if there is an impulse to formal propriety, even though chaos invades the situation where formal propriety puts a good face on murder. . . . the impulse to ritualisation is essential to the preserving of order.
>
>   (p. 159)

In contrast to this is Iago's killing of Emilia with the words 'Filth, thou liest', and this contrast is very relevant to the formality of the killings in early revenge plays and enforces their hieratic significance.

In the Genesis story it will be remembered that Cain's punishment is not death but exile; 'a wanderer shalt thou be in the earth. And Cain went out from the presence of the Lord.' It is of this judgement that Cain cries: 'my punishment

---

  * *Magic in the Web*, University of Kentucky Press, 1956.

is greater than I can bear'. His exile was strangely neglected in the early dramatisations of the myth. In *Locrine* 157, Humber, exiled and starving, strongly suggests Cain, as well as pointing forward to that later exile, Timon:

> Long have I lived in this desert cave,
> With eating haws and miserable roots,
> Devouring leaves and beastly excrements.
> Caves were my beds, and stones my pillow-bears,
> Fear was my sleep, and horror was my dream, . . .
> So that for fear and hunger, Humber's mind
> Can never rest, but always troubling stands.
>
> (*Locrine*, IV. 5. 1–11.)*

Shakespeare however uses this element of the story in the mature tragedies. Henry IV condemns Exton:

> With Cain go, wander through the shades of night.
>
> (*Richard II*, V.)

and four of the later heroes suffer Cain's doom. Macbeth's banishment from the world of humanity is complete. He is estranged from wife, friends and subjects, and he faces death utterly alone save for those who give:

> Curses, not loud but deep, Mouth-honour, breath
> Which the poor heart would fain deny, and dare not.   (V. 3.)

Lear is self-exiled:

> . . . I abjure all roofs, and choose
> To wage against the enmity of the air,
> To be a comrade with the wolf, and owl,
> Necessity's sharp pinch.   (II. 4.)

This is not the place to attempt to assess the full nature of

---

* Malone Society Reprint, Oxford, 1908; spelling modernised by the author.

Lear's guilt, but it resembles Cain's in so far as it destroys an intimate blood relationship—the driving out of Cordelia is indeed the sin of Cain, and possibly Lear survives in his exile because he has the mark of God upon him which makes his life sacred—the mark of madness.

Coriolanus is driven into exile by his fellow men, and in exile he is killed by his fellow men: the doom feared by Cain fell upon him. His punishment was indeed harder than he could bear; hence his failure to fulfil the laws of kind and his breach of the bonds of nature. He dies in the secular world of human history, where no God either condemns him or saves him from death. *Coriolanus* is a humanistic play; it has fewer overtones of hope in divine purpose or in transcendent goodness than any of Shakespeare's other mature plays; the passion of its later scenes springs from human hatred, human love and the treachery of a friend.

AUFIDIUS: Insolent villain

CONSPIRATORS: Kill, kill, kill, kill him.
   Draw . . . and kills Martius who falls, Aufidius stands on him.
                                                        (v. 6.)

When Aufidius stands with his foot on Coriolanus' breast, the exile has changed his role and become not the killer but the sacrifice, while his opponent momentarily becomes Cain. The last two speeches of the play leave the mind without any sense of reconciliation or hope. The Volscian Lord's words are pure opportunism; Aufidius's express only grief and absolute loss.

2ND LORD: His own impatience,
   Takes from Aufidius a great part of blame:
   Let's make the best of it.

AUFIDIUS: My rage is gone,
   And I am struck with sorrow. Take him up:
   . . . Though in this city he
   Hath widow'd and unchilded many a one . . .
   Yet he shall have a Noble Memory. Assist.   (v. 6.)

D

Timon of Athens, like Lear, is self-exiled:

> Let me look back upon thee. O thou Wall
> That girdles in those Wolves, dive in the earth,
> And fence not Athens. . . .
>   Nothing I'll bear from thee
> But nakedness, thou detestable town, . . .
> Timon will to the woods.   (IV. i.)

But the abandonment which he has elected to suffer becomes more than he can endure. At first he does not recognise this and takes pride in his refusal of his birthright of humanity.

ALCIBIADES: What art thou there? Speak.

TIMON: A beast as thou art. . . .

ALCIBIADES: What is thy name? Is man so hateful to thee,
    That art thyself a Man?

TIMON: I am Misanthropos, and hate mankind.
    For thy part, I could wish thou wert a dog,
    That I might love thee something.   (IV. 3.)

When he curses all that exists within the circling wall of Athens however, Timon calls down destruction not only on evil but on the very possibility of good:

> Piety, and Fear,
> Religion to the gods, Peace, Justice, Truth,
> Domestic awe, Night-rest, and Neighbourhood,
> Instruction, Manners, Mysteries, and Trades,
> Degrees, Observances, Customs, and Lawes,
> Decline to your confounding contraries,
> And let Confusion live.
>
>   (IV. 1.)

When such disciplines and observances do indeed decline to their 'confounding contraries', man enters the world of the 'absurd', the world without direction or purpose in which death remains the only reality. Timon finally enters this

world when he refuses the love of his one faithful friend, his
steward Flavius.

STEWARD: O let me stay, and comfort you, my Master.
TIMON: If thou hat'st curses
  Stay not.

(IV. 3.)

Apemantus bids Timon to 'Live and love thy misery', but
complete isolation means death:

> Timon hath made his everlasting Mansion
> Upon the Beached Verge of the salt Flood,
> Who once a day with his embossed Froth
> The turbulent Surge shall cover. . . .
> Lips, let sour words go by, and Language end:
> What is amiss, Plague and Infection mend.
> Graves only be men's works, and death their gain. (V. 2.)

Where isolation is accepted language may well end, for
communication becomes unnecessary, and death is indeed
man's only gain. In this world Timon dies, denying the
ordered universe which he had cursed.

As the plays of revenge by such dramatists as Tourneur,
Marston and Chettle became increasingly more horrific, plays
dealing with the forgiveness of wrongs suffered also increased
in number. Confidence in the righteousness of personal vengeance failed as certainly as the simple belief in the re-establishment of order by external means, and the theatre demonstrated the inadequacy of both conceptions. It also reflected the
search for a more Christian ethic. In Thomas Heywood's *A
Woman Killed with Kindness*,* Frankford, when he discovers
his wife's adultery with his friend Wendol, refrains in spite of
his grief from immediately avenging his honour:

> O God! O God! that it were possible
> To undo things done; to call back yesterday! . . .

* In *Four English Tragedies*, Penguin Books, 1953.

> But, oh! I talk of things impossible
> And cast beyond the moon.

(IV. 5.)

The lovers are surprised, and when he actually sees the man who has cuckolded him Frankford is again tempted to vengeance.

> (*Enter Wendol, running over the stage in a night-gown, he (Frankford) after him with his sword drawn; the maid in her smock stays his hand, and claps hold on him. He pauses for a while.*)

FRANKFORD: I thank thee maid; thou, like an angel's hand,
Hast stayed me from a bloody sacrifice.
Go villain, and my wrongs sit on thy soul
As heavy as this grief doth sit on mine!   (IV. 5.)

This mode of 'vengeance' proves potent. When Wendol reappears, he enters 'apart' and says:

> Pursued with horror of a guilty soul,
> And with the sharp scourge of repentance lashed,
> I fly from mine own shadow. . . .
> And I must now go wander like a Cain,
> In foreign countries and remotest climes,
> Where the report of my ingratitude
> Cannot be heard.

(XV. 3.)

The author's naturalism, successful enough in the earlier acts concerning the seduction and its discovery, proves inadequate to present the universal significance which it is to be presumed he intended his conclusion to carry. Act V, in which the repentant heroine starves herself to death before her forgiving husband and admiring friends, descends to a mawkish sentimentality which the formal convention of the earlier plays prevented.

Beside this may be placed a reminder of *Cymbeline*. This

play contains two attempted revenges, both of which are fore-
stalled. That of Cloten is presented in parody. His fetichism
in regard to Posthumus' clothes is not only psychologically
convincing but also makes a grotesque caricature of the demand
for vengeance which he himself considers dignified and proper.
Driven desperate by his uncouth pursuit of her and his dis-
paragement of her husband, Imogen at last taunts him:

IMOGEN: His mean'st Garment
   That ever hath but clipped his body; is dearer
   In my respect, than all the hairs above thee,
   Were they all made such men: . . . .

CLOTEN: His garments? Now the devil. . . .
   I'll be revenged:
   His mean'st Garment? Well.

(II. 3.)

When Imogen flees he decides to follow her:

She said upon a time (the bitterness of it, I now belch from my
heart) that she held the very Garment of Posthumus, in more
respect, than my noble and natural person; . . . With that suit upon
my back will I ravish her: . . . and when my Lust hath dined (which,
as I say, to vex her, I will execute in the Clothes that she so praised:)
to the Court, I'll knock her back, and foot her home again. . . . She
hath despised me rejoicingly, and I'll be merry in my Revenge.

(III. 5.)

Posthumus' demand for vengeance is potentially tragic;
when he believes it to have been fulfilled it is its own punishment:

Yea bloody cloth, I'll keep thee: for I wished
Thou shouldst be coloured thus. You married ones,
If each of you should take this course, how many
Must murder Wives much better than themselves
For wrying but a little? . . . .
            Gods, if you

> Should have ta'en vengeance on my faults, I never
> Had lived to put on this: so had you saved
> The noble Imogen to repent, and strook
> Me (wretch) more worth your Vengeance.   (v. 1.)

In his remorse he discards the clothes in which he had condemned Imogen and with them that aspect of himself which
had misjudged her.

> I'll disrobe me
> Of these Italian weeds, and suit myself
> As does a Britain peasant:—so I'll fight
> Against the part I come with: so I'll die
> For thee (O Imogen) even for whom my life
> Is every breath, a death.
>
>   (v. 1.)

He has thus forgiven Imogen for the wrong he believed she
did him before he learns he was mistaken, and, because he
has forgiven her, he is able to seek forgiveness for himself. In
captivity he finds first a new imprisonment and later a new
freedom:

> My Conscience, thou art fettered
> More than my shanks, and wrists: you good Gods give me
> The penitent Instrument to pick that Bolt,
> Then free for ever.
>
>   (v. 4.)

He can now forgive the real wrong he suffered, Iachimo's, as
he had previously forgiven the imagined one:

> Kneel not to me:
> The power that I have on you, is to spare you:
> The malice towards you, to forgive you.
>
>   (v. 5.)

We are now not far from the world of Prospero's Island where,
though the villain appears, the revenger is absent:

                    The rarer action is
In virtue than in vengeance: they being penitent,
The sole drift of my purpose doth extend
Not a frown further.   (v. 1.)

Shakespeare's treatment of the myth of the warring brothers
is not confined to the Elizabethan convention of revenge. In
King Lear, Edmund's three-fold trumpet challenge answered
by the mysterious, distant call of Edgar's music, introduces
what is perhaps the supreme theatrical reflection of the fratricidal strife of good and evil, but here the myth is used in
reverse; the duel is a true mirror image. The challenge was
Abel's, not Cain's. Edgar has approached this climactic moment
slowly, ever since he moved off the heath with Lear and the
Fool, who sang of Childe Roland at the Dark Tower, a hero of
folk-lore far older than the Christian mythos. When the
battle is finally joined it is Cain who dies, so that our attention
is directed not to Good Friday but to the final victory of Easter
Sunday. If this was Shakespeare's intention he may well have
been remembering that the 'vengeance' of God becomes man's
salvation. In his essay on Hamlet,* Christopher Devlin has
demonstrated the use in Elizabethan Roman Catholic literature of the word 'revenge' as the equivalent of purgation, e.g.
'And look how much matter there is left in their sinnes . . . so
much all the punishments of this fire revenge.' † Father
Devlin also quotes Cardinal Allen: '. . . shall we doubt of God's
justice in the perfect revenge of sin in the soul or purifying
that nature which . . . appertaineth to the . . . glory ever-
lasting'.‡ Edmund dies, but not before he has craved Edgar's
forgiveness and attempted to save Lear and Cordelia. It is
possible therefore that Shakespeare conceived of Edgar's act
as being both punitive and redemptive: 'the perfect revenge'
which purifies and does not destroy.

In *The Tempest* Shakespeare presents one last pair of

* *Hamlet's Divinity*, Hart-Davis, 1963.
† Parsons, *Christian Directory*, 1650, p. 365.
‡ Allen, *A Defence of Purgatory*, Antwerp, 1565, p. 592.

brothers, and here again the struggle ends in the victory of
'Abel'. Antonio, the 'Cain', does indeed achieve his brother's
symbolic death by water, but it is only to face him, risen, on
the shores of the island which is, in one sense, Paradise. But
whereas Edgar and Edmund 'exchange charity', Prospero and
Antonio do not, for when Antonio is offered forgiveness for his
'rankest fault', he makes no reply. Perhaps Shakespeare hints
that the time for reconciliation may pass. In *The Tempest* the
young achieve happiness, but only the old who can accept this
with vicarious rejoicing, can find reconciliation and content.

The world of George Chapman is an ordered but not a
specifically Christian one, and his attitude to vengeance is
therefore bound to be different from any considered hitherto.
His plays have lost the primitive innocence and naïve belief in
the triumph of goodness which characterised the popular
drama and informed the literary work of writers in the main
stream of the Christian tradition. Both plays about Bussy
d'Ambois are essentially non-Christian; their values are humanistic, and the most explicitly religious lines refer to no Christian
saint but to the pagan, Antigone:

> Nor would she value Creon's written laws
> With God's unwritten edicts.
> (*Revenge of Bussy D'Ambois*, II. 2, p. 252).*

Bussy denies the validity of all such laws; his conception of
man's position in the universe is that of Chapman's later hero,
Byron who cries:

> . . . be free, all worthy spirits,
> And stretch yourselves, for greatness and for height:
> Untruss your slaveries: you have height enough
> Beneath this steep Heaven to use all your reaches;
> 'Tis too far off to let you or respect you.
> Give me a spirit that on this life's rough sea
> Loves t' have his sails fill'd with the lusty wind,
> Even till his sail-yards tremble, his masts crack,

* Chapman, ed. Phelps, Mermaid Series, Benn, 1895.

And his rapt ship run on her side so low
That she drinks water, and her keel plows the air.
There is no danger to a man that knows
What life and death is; there's not any law
Exceeds his knowledge; neither is it lawful
That he should stoop to any other law.
He goes before them, and commands them all,
That to himself is a law rational.

(*The Conspiracy of Charles, Duke of Byron*, iii. 1. p. 372.)

Man is not to Chapman a fallen being but the glory of the universe:

The evil man. . . .
. . . resisting th' All is crushed with it,
But he, that knowing how divine a frame
The whole world is; and of it all, can name,
Without self-flattery, no part so divine
As he himself, and therefore will confine
Freely, his whole powers, in his proper part,
Goes on most godlike.

(*Revenge of Bussy D'Ambois*, iii. i. p. 274.)

Bussy asserts his dignity as a man and demands a place in the 'establishment' equal to his merit and on a par with that of its leaders of noble birth. He does not threaten to destroy the hierarchical society, but he asserts himself within it by completely amoral means, that is to say by adultery and duelling. When as a result of his challenge he is murdered, his ghost demands vengeance of his brother, but this vengeance when it comes cannot correctly be seen as punishment for sin. These plays are bounded by human society; they are deeply concerned with ethics but not in any sincere way with the supernatural or with religious values.

Bussy, in the Christian world, merited the punishment he received as an adulterer and a murderer, and even in the social world of courtesy and honour he owed satisfaction to the husband whom he had disgraced. He is killed primarily because he is a social upstart, and his enemies turn against him the same amoral philosophy that he employs against them. He is clearly as acceptable to his creator, in spite of all his arrogance and predatory sexuality, as his counterparts in much modern drama are to theirs. His values are those of the individualist; if he is to be revenged the vengeance is an assertion of anarchy not of order or justice.

Clermont d'Ambois hesitates long before avenging his brother and endeavours to take his decision on rational grounds. In argument with their vindictive and passionate sister, Charlotte, he states the reasons for his reluctance:

CLERMONT: Shall we revenge a villainy with villainy?

CHARLOTTE: Is it not equal?

CLERMONT: Shall we be equal with villains?
　Is that your reason?
　We must wreak our wrongs
　So that we make* not more
　Nor can we call it virtue that proceeds
　From vicious fury . . . .

(The Revenge of Bussy D'Ambois, III. i. p. 265.)

He does at last challenge and kill his brother's murderer, within the socially accepted framework of the duel, but Chapman places all the emphasis of the play's conclusion on a different conception. Clermont is never presented as a 'justicer' of God, and although he avenges only at the price of his own life, as do the Christian avengers, the motivation of his death is different from theirs. It is quite divorced from the killing of his brother's murderers. Among the ghosts who rise from the land of the dead to accept the sacrifice of Montsurry's life, Clermont recognises his friend and master the duke of Guise. When he understands that this man is dead, he follows him by a death in love, quite separate from his achievement of vengeance on the body of his enemy:

　　　Guise, O my lord, how shall I cast from me
　　　The bands and coverts hindering me from thee?

* Emendation of 'take'.

The garments or the cover of the mind,
The human soul is; of the soul, the spirit
The proper robe is; of the spirit, the blood;
And of the blood the body is the shroud;
With that I must begin then to unclothe
And come to th'other. Now then as a ship,
Touching at strange and far-removed shores;
Her men ashore go, for their several ends,
Fresh water, victuals, precious stones, and pearl,
All yet intentive (when the master calls
The ship to put off ready) to leave all
Their greediest labours, lest they there be left
To thieves, or beasts, or be the country's slaves:
So, now my master calls, . . .
. . . shall I here survive,
Not cast me after him into the sea,
Rather than here to live, ready every hour
To feed thieves, beasts, and be the slave of power?
I come my lord, Clermont thy creature comes.

                                    (v. 1. pp. 315–16.)

This is poetry of the highest order, but it is the poetry of a
world where the only positive values lie in personal relationships and personal loyalties. Chapman's is not an anarchic
world for it contains a system of ethical values, but it is not a
world where individuals are bound to submit to either a divine
or a social law; it is no more the world of Marx than that of
Dante, of Brecht than that of Shakespeare. The climactic
speech is a brilliant piece of romantic individualism. The plots
and action of the plays, however, fail clearly to illuminate
their real centre—individuals adrift in a godless and therefore
an unconcerned world, and the conflict between the older faith
in God and the new faith in man is not conveyed in a fully
satisfactory way. They offer no answer to the plea:

O real Goodness, if thou be a power,
And not a word alone, in humane uses,
Appear out of this angry conflagration.
(*Tragedy of Charles, Duke of Byron*, v. 1. p. 469.)

CHAPTER 2

THE TRIUMPH OF EVIL:
Some Jacobean Revenge Plays

'Tis not a shallow probe
Can search this ulcer soundly; I fear you'll find it
Full of corruption.

THOMAS MIDDLETON, *The Changeling*

THESE words of Thomas Middleton serve well as an introduction to the revenge plays of the seventeenth century for in reading or watching them we enter a new and more sinister world, where evil is all powerful, and where goodness, when it shines at all, flickers fitfully, only to be extinguished. The authors of these plays, particularly Webster, Middleton and Ford, have, in their work as artists, lost all sense of the order which was finally vindicated even in the work of the sombre humanist, Chapman. In this they reflect an obsession of their age, whose tormented concern with evil has probably not been equalled since until the third quarter of the twentieth century. Horror at the world in which they found themselves is expressed in seventeenth-century man's fascinated and bestial concern with witchcraft. The geographical extent of this shows that the disease was common to the whole of Western Christian society, and not confined to Protestant countries, where the loss of hope given by belief in penance and purgatory, may have joined with the Genevan terrors of predestination or the Lutheran obsession with power of the devil to inflame men's imagination of evil. The cult of witchcraft is of particular interest in relation to Middleton's work, as he shows a peculiar awareness of the disintegration of the personality which a willed and continued association with evil can bring, a disintegration to be seen in the confessions of many a self-accused witch.

These plays are closely associated with the break-down of faith in an ordered universe which gives its peculiar quality to the twentieth-century 'theatre of the absurd', where anything is possible because nothing can be understood or expected. In this godless world men neither hope nor seek for an absolute revelation of value; they pursue petty avocations with such attention, enthusiastic or lackadaisical as their temperaments dictate. The contrast between this and earlier days is pithily expressed in Bosola's comments on the tombs of princes:

> Princes' images on their tombs do not lie, as they were wont, seemingly to pray up to Heaven; but with their hands under their cheeks, as if they died of the toothache; they are not carved with their eyes fixed upon the stars; but as their minds were wholly bent upon the world, the self-same way they seem to turn their faces.
>
> (*The Duchess of Malfi*, IV. 2.)

In the source from which Middleton draws the plot of *The Changeling* the material is presented in the old orthodox manner, stressing the miraculous quality of the self-betrayal of the murderess. Of the heroine it says: 'Loe, the providence of God so ordained it, that she is reduced to this exigent and extremity, as she must be a witness against herself, and in seeking to conceal her whoredom, must discover her murder.' *

The play itself still carries some traces of the revenge tradition with its Christian implications: the murdered man's ghost returns (but he visits the murderers, not the revenger); Beatrice-Joanna, as in the source material, betrays herself by confessing her share in the murder to clear herself of the charge of adultery, and the murdered man's brother and avenger has only to wait in order to see the murderers dead at his feet. Nevertheless the power of the play comes from quite other sources. There is nothing to suggest the supernatural in the destruction of Beatrice-Joanna. It follows her own actions inevitably in a world where evil is stronger than good, or at

* *The Triumphs of God's Revenge Against Murder*, Reynolds, 1621, quoted in *The Changeling*, ed. N. W. Bawcutt, The Revels Series, appendix A, p. 126.

least than innocence. Beatrice-Joanna at the beginning of the play is like Eve, knowing neither good nor evil. She is cold towards her affianced husband, de Piracquo, and when she finds herself in love with Alsemero she decides to get rid of her betrothed. Her instincts are those of a young animal without scruple or thought of the future. She acts, and her action destroys her. No super-human power exists able to save her or even feel interest in her downfall. She invokes evil, and the power of evil is irresistible. Lady Macbeth calls explicitly on the spirits that wait on mortal thoughts; there is no need for them in *The Changeling*. Human nature itself supplies the tool of destruction, the motive and the means.

da Flores, the ugly, uncouth gentleman-at-arms, is a typical 'outsider'. At odds with society, he owes it nothing and hardly regrets, certainly is not surprised at, the meagre rewards it offers his services. He is an individualist; his one passionate desire is to enjoy the apparently untouchable princess, Beatrice-Joanna. When she sees in him a possible means to the removal of the obstacle to her marriage, she overcomes her physical repulsion at his presence with a kind of gloating which makes his later attraction for her completely convincing both on a psychological and a metaphysical level. Once she has stretched out her hand to the apple, so longed for and so loathed, the canker spreads over her as insidiously and irresistibly as leprosy. The famous dialogue in Act III. 4 reaches its climax thus:

DA FLORES: I have eased you
   Of your trouble, think on it; I am in pain,
   And must be eased of you; 'tis a charity,
   Justice invites your blood to understand me.

BEATRICE: I dare not.

DA FLORES: Quickly!

BEATRICE: O I never shall! . . .
   Why, 'tis impossible thou shouldst be so wicked,
   Or shelter such a cunning cruelty,
   To make his death the murderer of my honour! . . .

DA FLORES: Pash! you forget yourself; . . .
  Look but into your conscience, read me there;
  'Tis a true book, you'll find me there your equal:
  Pash! fly not to your birth, but settle you
  In what the act has made you; you're no more now.
  You must forget your parentage to me;
  You are the deed's creature; by that name
  You lost your first condition, and I challenge you,
  As peace and innocency has turned you out,
  And made you one with me.

                           (III. 4.)

da Flores is right; she soon gives way to him entirely, so that
even of her wedding night he can say to her bridegroom:

      the while I coupled with your mate
  At barley-break; now we are left in hell.

VERSEMERO: We are all there, it circumscribes us here (v. 3.)

She learns the truth about herself only in death, and neither
husband, father, priest nor any friend offers help or sheds a
tear for her; only da Flores, her evil angel, pities her.

BEATRICE: *(to her father)*
  O, come not near me, sir, I shall defile you!
  I that am of your blood was taken from you
  For your better health; look no more upon't
  But cast it to the ground regardlessly:
  Let the common sewer take it from distinction. . . .

DA FLORES: I loved this woman in spite of her heart . . .
  Make haste, Joanna. . . .
  I would not go to leave thee far behind.

The murdered man's brother accepts these deaths as a righteous
vengeance for Piracquo's death. They are indeed indissolubly
linked to it by cause and effect. Both the practical and the
psychological results of the murder have brought its perpe-
trators to this end. No ghost was needed to call for vengeance;

it came without calling. No ritualisation was desired that it
might dignify the dreadful consequences of dreadful deeds.
Yet Tomaso de Piracquo's words fall somewhat coldly and un-
pleasantly upon the ear:

> Sir, I am satisfied; my injuries
> Lie dead before me; I can exact no more,
> Unless my soul were loose, and could o'ertake
> Those black fugitives that are fled from hence,
> To take a second vengeance; but there are wraths
> Deeper than mine, 'tis to be feared about 'em.

(v. 3.)

One of the rare supernatural references in the play is thus to
hell, but the words seem supererogatory; the sense of absolute
loss has already been conveyed–Versemero's line was true; a
hell on earth does indeed circumscribe the human chaos of this
disordered world. The characters who remain make a sad
attempt to console each other

> Sir, you have yet a son's duty living,
> Please you accept it; let that your sorrow
> As it goes from your eye, go from your heart;
> Man and his sorrow at the grave must part.

(v. 3.)

On this purely humanistic note the play ends.

In *Women Beware Women** Middleton has created a close-
knit group of characters who through their own greed, lust,
pride, or merely their love of meddling and their blindness,
betray, torture and destroy each other exactly as human
beings did in Florence and in London when the play was
written. Livia, the middle-aged widow who spoils her young
lover, and allows him to hide the shame of his cuckoldry under
the fine clothes given him by his elderly mistress, Isabel and
Hippolito who indulge their perverse love making simpler
folk their lackeys, the old woman who betrays her trust for the

* *Select Plays*, Mermaid Series, 1887.

sake of a gossip and a game of chess, the elderly lecher who
defies society and marries his young mistress, all are familiar
human figures, and all sow the seeds of the destruction they
will surely reap. Bianca, at the beginning of the play, is as
innocent as was Beatrice-Joanna, and she changes as completely. From the happy young bride, pleased with all she sees,
she becomes the petulant, spoiled beauty who thinks the best is
only her due and finally decides to poison the man who she
fears may deprive her of it. All this is credible enough, and it
fills four acts of the play. What it is impossible to believe of
these people, as natural and convincing as Ibsen's characters,
is that they would organise a masque at which Cupids shot
poisoned arrows, at which a suspended goddess was killed by
the fumes of incense, and someone fell through a trap-door
on to a caltrop laid for his enemy, while poisoned cups were
offered by goddesses to the onlookers. Yet this is exactly the
subject-matter of Act v. Here Kyd's ritualisation of vengeance
becomes merely a device by which certain characters seek to
achieve their personal ends. Without its old supernatural associations it proves a clumsy and unconvincing piece of plotting
which marks the ultimate degradation of the revenge convention. Middleton would have written a far better play if he had
forgotten his theories about suitable means for punishing wrong
doings and been content to notice and dramatise the actual
progress from evil to destruction as he did in *The Changeling*.
His work offers a severe, even Puritanical, but negative
morality. His universe is still one in which the breach of its
laws means death, and in this limited sense he shows Justice
to be achieved with a measure of certainty.

In the world of John Webster's plays we are not faced with
the spectacle of goodness being corrupted by evil and thus
ensuring its own destruction. There are figures of real goodness in Webster's plays, but they remain pitifully weak, and
still uncorrupted they are swept to destruction by forces of evil
outside themselves. Both *The White Devil* and *The Duchess of
Malfi* show vestiges of the original revenge convention, but
their power lies in their sombre poetry and psychological

E

expertise, and neither retains a jot of the faith in the inevitable re-establishment of the divine order which that convention was designed to convey.

In *The White Devil** Isabella's silvery purity and Marcello's youthful integrity are as defenceless as is the complacent fatuity of Camillo, when they stand in the way of Vittoria's passion or Flamineo's ambition. The only values which appear to have a chance of survival in the evil which surrounds them are the humanistic ones of abounding vitality and a passion for life. This intensity of living, this outrageous defiance of society in the name of desire are what redeem the relationship of Vittoria and Brachiano from sordidness and triviality. These two are among the earliest, as they are among the most ruthless, of the individualists who fight for the right to live and love exempt from the rule of a society which means nothing to them. They fight with filthy weapons, nevertheless they fight in a cause which has had upholders more admirable, though not more genuine, than they. They pay a price which is a just one according to the orthodox morality of the society in which they live, but those who exact the penalty are lesser beings than they: no justicers of a divine order but treacherous, self-seeking and sadistic egoists.

The act of vengeance is presented as a scabrous parody of the ritual of the masque or dance of the older plays and also of the ritual of the Church. Brachiano is actually killed by poison sprinkled in his tilting helmet, but for the final ceremony he is 'presented in a bed', and Gasparo and Lodovico, disguised 'in the habit of Capuchins, present him with a crucifix and hallowed candle' and continue with a vicious mockery of the Church's consolation to the dying. Later these avengers, who claim that they have their 'vows sealed with the sacrament', secretly, 'the rest being departed . . . discover themselves':

GASPARO: Brachiano!

LODOVICO: Devil Brachiano,
   Thou art damned.

* John Webster, *Collected Works*, ed. F. L. Lucas, vol. 1.

GASPARO: Perpetually . . .
  This is Count Lodovico.

LODOVICO: This Gasparo.
  And thou shalt die like a poore rogue.

GASPARO: And stinke
  Like a dead, flie-blowne dog.

LODOVICO: And be forgotten before thy funeral sermon.

BRACHIANO: Vittoria! Vittoria!   (v. 3.)

Brachiano's cry stems from a level of anguish deeper than
anything inherent in the avengers' masquerade, yet after it
the action once more returns to the old ritual with its presentation of a gift to the magnate in whose honour the masque was
produced:

LODOVICO: You would prate Sir? This is a true-love knot,
  Sent from the Duke of Florence.

  (*He strangles Brachiano.*)

GASPARO: What, is it done?

LODOVICO: The snuff is out. No woman-keeper in the world,
  Though she had practis'd seven years at the pest-house,
  Could have done it quaintlyer.   (v. 3.)

Even the self-congratulation on the method of the killing runs
true to tradition.

The final vengeance is the killing of Vittoria in revenge of
Brachiano's murdered wife, Isabella. It is this which is called
by Francisco, when he deputes Lodovico to achieve it, 'this
glorious act', and for the doing of which he promises the perpe-
trator lasting fame. In planning it Francisco abandons even a
pretence at righteousness. After Zanche's confession of her and
Vittoria's connivance at the murders of Isabella and Camillo,
Lodovico says:

  Why now our action's justified.

But Francisco returns:

> Tush for Justice!
> What harmes it Justice? we now, like the partridge,
> Purge the disease with lawrell, for the fame
> Shall crowne the enterprise and quit the shame. (v. 3.)

It is this second murder which is introduced with an explicit reference to the pattern of the older plays. The revengers enter Vittoria's room with their faces hidden:

LODOVICO: We have brought you a maske.

FLAMINEO: A matachine it seemes
By your drawn swords. . . .

CONSPIRATORS: Isabella! Isabella!

LODOVICO: Doe you know us now? . . .

FLAMINEO: You shall not take Justice from forth my hands.
O let me kill her! (v. 6.)

But this is not allowed; the pattern of the ritual killing is to continue; Flamineo is among its destined victims and may not be an executioner.

GASPARO: Bind him to the pillar. . . .

LODOVICO: Sirrah, you once did strike me, I'll strike you
Into the centre.

FLAMINEO: Thou'lt do it like a hangman; a base hangman,
Not like a noble fellow, for thou seest
I cannot strike again. (v. 6.)

The physical violence is nakedly hideous; the sword-dance, the matachin, is no longer a stylisation of justice, and Flamineo is right when he calls the avengers common hangmen.

In *The Duchess of Malfi* the recollections of the revenge convention are not so apparent, and indeed their traces might not be noticed at all if it were not for Bosola's explicit statement when the bodies of Ferdinand and the Cardinal are discovered.

RODERIGO: How comes this?

BOSOLA: Revenge for the Duchess of Malfi murdered
   By the Arrogonian brethren; for Antonio
   Slain by this hand; for lustful Julia
   Poisoned by this man, and lastly for myself
   That was an actor in the main of all
   Much 'gainst my own good nature. (v. 5.)

There has been no disguising here, but surely recollection of its old uses gives additional justification and a clearer meaning to those stabbings in the night. They take place in a darkness which is a disguise more effective than any masks or revellers' robes could be, and which allows the violence of the revengers full scope. There follows the new ironic twist, for this is no world in which 'the secret purposes' of God will be effected by the hands of men, but one where 'ignorant armies clash by night'; a world in which Bosola kills the man he most wished to save and himself dies in a mist.

   I know not how: such a mistake as I
   Have often seen in a play. (v. 5.)

Webster writes of a world which has indeed become 'absurd'. There is of course another vengeance exacted in *The Duchess of Malfi* which acts as a kind of anti-masque to the righteous, though belated, vengeance achieved by Bosola; this masque is presented with the traditional purpose that it should destroy the noble person in whose honour it takes place. The revenge plotted by Ferdinand for the imaginary wrong his honour has sustained is itself the original true wrong which is finally avenged by Bosola. To the duchess, sitting in her 'last presence chamber', there enters a servant. He begins by saying:

   I am come to tell you
   Your brother hath intended you some sport, (IV. 2.)

and he goes on to introduce the madmen whom Ferdinand is
sending her. She accepts them formally, like the great lady she
is:

> Let them come in . . .
> Sit Cariola. Let them loose when you please
> For I am chained to endure all your tyranny.   (IV.2.)

The madmen sing and dance grotesquely, until there enters
Bosola, standing like Comus among his rout, with, but not of,
his grotesque fellows. Bosola plays the part of Death, and he
presents to the duchess the gift which had become essential to
the ritual of a court masque. It is a 'coffin, cords and a bell'
carried in by the two executioners.

BOSOLA: Here is a present from your princely brothers,
  And may it arrive welcome, for it brings
  Last benefit, last sorrow.   (IV. 2.)

The duchess dies in the faith that her executioners will 'pull
down heaven' upon her, but there is nothing in the play to
confirm this. 'The stars shine still', but no music of the spheres
is audible. In *The Duchess of Malfi* there remain the last
remnants of such a metaphysical order. Goodness is helpless to
defend itself, but evil is equally so. Its triumph is an illusion,
for it is ultimately self-destructive. In its last act the play
becomes a riot of lust, madness and confusion; the colourless
words of Delio, concerning the duchess's surviving son, are
nothing more than a token payment to the convention of a
happy ending. The memories of goodness in Webster's universe serve only to create a confusion, an ambivalence, missing
in Middleton's more consistently sombre and materialistic
one. In Webster's plays a divine order lies in ruins, but goodness remains beautiful, and its beauty is recognised even by its
destroyers, so that an admission of inferiority is wrung from
the depths of their despair:

> Cover her face; mine eyes dazzle.
>   (IV. 2.)

The beauty of the duchess, though it is her beauty in death, remains precious, while the hideousness of evil is conveyed by the sight of Ferdinand snarling and twisting in his lycan-thropy and by the image in the fishpond of the Cardinal's bitter self-knowledge:

> a thing armed with a rake
> That seems to strike at me.
>
> (v. 5.)

The writer who can bring us closest to the world as Webster here saw it is no contemporary of his own but Soren Kierke-gaard, who in the nineteenth century, when the old religious values were dissolving around him, analysed man's sense of sin and guilt in the *Concept of Dread*.* He might have been picturing Ferdinand when he writes that 'the demoniacal becomes thoroughly evident only when it is touched by the good' (p. 106) and describes examples of the brutish nature gaining such an ascendancy over a man that it makes itself known by:

inarticulate animal sounds or by mimicry of animal ways and a brutish look, whether it be that brutishness acquires in man a pronounced form . . . or in a flash, like a disappearing express, it suggests a presentiment of what dwells within, as the glance or gesture of a madman in the space of an instant which is shorter than the blink of an eye, parodies, mocks, caricatures the sensible, dis-creet, intelligent man with whom one is talking.

In John Ford's greatest play, *'Tis Pity She's a Whore*, the sense of our irrational world is stronger than in any work by Webster. Stronger perhaps than in that of any succeeding dramatist before Strindberg, its peculiar note is occasionally like a pre-echo of the voice heard in Kafka's novels. In what is thought to be his first tragedy, however, his world view is very close to Webster's. In *The Broken Heart* (1633)† Orgilus, who

* Trans. W. Lowrie, Oxford, 1947, p. 105.
† Dent, Everyman's Library, 899, *Webster and Ford*, ed. G. B. Harrison.

is betrothed to Penthea, seeks vengeance on her brother, Ithocles, who has prevented their union and given his sister to a jealous nonentity. The two were deeply in love, and Orgilus considers their betrothal as binding as a marriage.

> I would possess my wife; the equity
> Of very reason bids me.   (II. 3.)

The play shows every sympathy with this, but Orgilus' revenge is an orgy of treacherous cruelty. Ithocles, who, when he falls in love himself, sincerely repents his earlier behaviour and seeks Orgilus' forgiveness and friendship, comes to mourn over his dead sister, is trapped in a mechanical chair and so stabbed to death. But the horror of the chair is not mere sensationalism; Ithocles is held fast by his own deeds as inescapably as by his friend's perverse cruelty. The chair is a mantrap in which we see him caught, like Laertes, in his 'own springe', held as helpless as Strindberg's Captain in his straitjacket. The significance of each man's helplessness is, however, different. In *The Father* the hero is the victim of the wickedness of others. His own strength is first sapped and then turned against him by the women whom he has loved and who betray him; he is shown rather as a martyr than as a man justly punished. Ithocles on the other hand is the prisoner of his own past, from which, however much he regrets it, he cannot escape. In *The Broken Heart* goodness is indeed unprotected, but evil is still punished in a world whose order can be seen and recognised by human reason. Orgilus pays the price due as well as his victim. He is not satisfied by Ithocles' death; his enemy's betrothed, Calantha, must die also, so that two lives may quit his and Penthea's buried love. Here there are vestigial traces of Kyd's old formula, for Orgilus is asked by the King to provide a masque at court and consents, but instead of a play we watch the famous dance, between 'the changes' of which Orgilus and his accomplices bring to the princess the news of the deaths first of her father, then of Penthea and finally of Ithocles, while she continues to lead the

dance until it is completed. This shock causes her death, so that
Orgilus' revenge is consummated during a formal ritual, but
the ritual is in no way used to de-personalise—still less to
justify—his actions. Calantha's first act as queen is to condemn
the revenger to death for the murder of Ithocles, and he dies
with the conventional admission of the divine justice of his
punishment but with the awareness and acceptance of spiritual
destruction which Ford's characters share only with Webster's
and occasionally Shakespeare's:

> Oh, Tecnicus, inspired by Phoebus' fire!
> I call to mind thy orgury, 'twas perfect;
> *Revenge proves its own executioner . . . .**
> A mist hangs o'er mine eyes, the sun's bright splendour
> Is clouded with an everlasting shadow:
> Welcome thou ice that sit'st about my heart,
> No heat can ever thaw thee.   (v. 2.)

Othello can be imagined as voicing such thoughts, and his loss
was like that of Orgilus, the loss of what seemed to each man a
perfect love.

Calantha goes on to arrange the succession and ensure order
in the kingdom, before—at her coronation ceremony—she dies
herself.

> Oh, my lords,
> I but deceived your eyes with antic gesture,
> When one news straight came huddling on another,
> Of death! and death! and death! still I danced forward,
> But it struck home;
> They are the silent griefs that cut the heartstrings;
> Let me die smiling.
>   (v. 3.)

This murder by mental torture is perhaps the most subtle
of all the murders for vengeance, as it is also the most

* Italics Ford's.

completely removed from any conception of justice. The play
ends with attention concentrated on the dead lovers, Calantha
and Ithocles, who are left in a kind of pale triumph, for the
play's final statement is that both peace and love can only be
found in death.

Dirge

Crowns may flourish and decay,
Beauties shine but fade away,
Youth may revel, yet it must
Lie down in a bed of dust.
Earthly honours flow and waste,
Time alone doth change and last.
Sorrows mingled with contents, prepare
          Rest from care:
Love only reigns in death; though art
Can find no comfort for a broken heart.

(v. 3.)

The echoes of Fidele's dirge only serve to emphasise the
difference between Ford's tacit acceptance of death as fulfilment and Shakespeare's unshaken dependence on the return
of life and spring.

In *'Tis Pity She's a Whore** there is again much talk of
revenge while the emotional centre of the play lies elsewhere.
The crime is a love between brother and sister, but it is
expressed with a simplicity and a depth of emotion which
make of it a satisfactory symbol of any love which breaches
the social code. The Friar calls Giovanni 'castaway', and the
boy himself admits at first the guilt of his passion:

Lost! I am lost! my fates have doom'd my death:
The more I strive, I love; the more I love
The less I hope: I see my ruin certain . . .
          What wit or art
Could counsel I have practised, but alas!
          I am still the same.

(i. 3.)

* Dent, Everyman's Library, 899. *Webster and Ford.*

Ford presents this literally fatal passion with an absence of moral judgement as complete as is his sympathy.

GIOVANNI: And here's my breast; strike home! . . .
  Why stand you?

ANNABELLA: Are you earnest?

GIOVANNI: Yes, most earnest,
  You cannot love?

ANNABELLA: Whom?

GIOVANNI: Me.

The simplicity of the language makes an irresistible appeal such as is heard again in the ritual vows of the lovers.

ANNABELLA: For every sigh that you have spent for me,
  I have sighed ten; for every tear, shed twenty;
  And not so much for that I loved, as that
  I durst not say I loved, nor scarcely think it . . .
  On my knees,
  Brother, even by our mother's dust, I charge you,
  Do not betray me to your mirth or hate;
  Love me or kill me, brother.

GIOVANNI: On my knees,
  Sister, even by our mother's dust, I charge you,
  Do not betray me to your mirth or hate;
  Love me, or kill me, sister.

                                                    (I. 3.)

To hide their love Annabella finally marries Soranzo, and it is he, with his henchman Vasquez, who plans and achieves vengeance. Again vestigial remains of the old convention are found in the plot. Soranzo's life is threatened by his discarded mistress, Hippolita, who presents a masque at his wedding and is tricked into drinking herself from the poisoned cup she intended to present to him.

VASQUEZ: Foolish woman, thou art now like a firebrand, that hath kindled others and burnt thyself . . . as for life, there's no hope, think not on it.

OMNES: Wonderful justice!

RICHARDETTO: Heaven, thou art righteous.

HIPPOLITA: Oh 'tis true,
I feel my minute coming.

(IV. 1.)

This is but peripheral material, however, and Soranzo's true revenge, when it comes, is brutal gang violence and reminds one of the killing of Hector by Achilles.* First Annabella's confidante, Putana, is mutilated and blinded, and then Giovanni is invited to Soranzo's home where bandits are hidden in readiness for his murder. Soranzo and Vasquez both fight with Giovanni, and when Soranzo falls Vasquez gives the agreed signal to the hired thugs.

VASQUEZ: I shall fit you anon—VENGEANCE!

(*The Bandits rush in.*)

GIOVANNI: Welcome! Come more of you; what e'er you be I dare your worst—

(*They surround and wound him.*)

VASQUEZ: Now you are *welcome*, sir—away, my masters all is done; shift for yourselves, your reward is your own; shift for yourselves.

BANDITS: Away, away!

Giovanni dies with a joy in death like Calantha's.

CARDINAL: Think of thy life and end, and call for mercy.

GIOVANNI: Mercy? why I have found it in this justice.

CARDINAL: Strive yet to cry to Heaven.

GIOVANNI: Oh, I bleed fast.
Death, thou art a guest long look'd for, I embrace

* Shakespeare, *Troilus and Cressida*, v. 9.

Thee and thy wounds; oh, my last minute comes!
Where 'er I go, let me enjoy this grace,
Freely to view my Annabella's face.

DONADO: Strange miracle of justice!

The two voices in which the same word 'justice' is uttered are
deliberately contrasted: Giovanni's sardonically sceptical, Donado's childishly complacent. Society, however cynically, accepts
Donado's view and allows Giovanni's murderer to go free.
Donado again comments: "'Tis most just', but justice could
hardly be more bitterly denigrated. The parting words of
Giovanni and Annabella show to what different values the
play subscribes. As their story reaches its climax they both
know that death must be imminent, and the woman is willing
to go on living in the present moment ignoring the inevitable
future, although the man cannot do so.

ANNABELLA: Brother, dear brother, know what I have been,
    And know that now there's but a dining-time
    'Twixt us and our confusion; let's not waste
    Those precious hours in vain and useless speech . . .
                Be not deceived, my brother,
    This banquet is an harbinger of death
    To you and me.

In one of those still and timeless moments before calamity the
brother and sister speak of the end of the world, and perhaps it
is his sister's words which give Giovanni in his last minutes, in
spite of his own scepticism, a hope of seeing her again.

GIOVANNI: But 'twere somewhat strange
    To see the waters burn; could I believe
    This might be true, I could believe as well
    There might be hell or heaven.

ANNABELLA: That's most certain.

GIOVANNI: A dream, a dream! else in this other world
    We should know one another.

ANNABELLA: So we shall.

GIOVANNI: Have you heard so?

ANNABELLA: For certain. . . .

GIOVANNI: Look up, look here; what see you in my face?

ANNABELLA: Distraction and a troubled conscience.

GIOVANNI: Death, and a swift repining wrath:—yet look,
  What see you in mine eyes?

ANNABELLA: Methinks you weep.

Again it is the simplicity of the monosyllables that carries the words to the heart. Ford clearly accepts the vagaries of human emotion, but he has little hope that freedom for its indulgence will bring happiness. Giovanni at first wonders at his own liberty from social prejudice:

> Busy opinion is an idle fool,
> That as a school-rod keeps a child in awe,
> Frights th'unexperienced temper of the mind:
> So did it me.

Later he is proud that such fears are overcome:

> Oh the glory
> Of two united hearts like hers and mine!
> My world and all of happiness is here,
> And I'd not change it for the best to come.
>
> (v. 3.)

That the happiness is fleeting only increases our sympathy with it. Vasquez, when he first hears of the incest, remarks: 'To what a height of liberty in damnation hath the devil trained our age.' (IV. 3.) If anyone has achieved 'liberty in damnation' it might be himself, but the play does not suggest that there is any power which will exact the penalty, for these characters move in an irrational world. In seeking the 'good' of their love Giovanni and Annabella have been driven to

destroy, first, other 'goods', and at last their love itself. Annabella married Soranzo to betray and cuckold him, and when
Giovanni at last faced their persecutor with her bleeding heart
upon the point of his dagger, he had not destroyed her more
certainly than their love had already done. Life in society left
no path of goodness open to them. In Professor Ribner's words:
'the tragedy of Ford's heroes and heroines is their inability to
find a satisfactory alternative to sin'. * Ford is in fact approaching the existentialist world in which men must create and
fulfil their own purposes or else live in the midst of absurdity.
The Friar threatens Giovanni, who has admitted his love for
his sister, Annabella, with the inevitable punishment of sin,
in terms of the age that was passing:

FRIAR: But Heaven is angry, and be thou resolved,
   Thou art a man remark'd to taste a mischief.
   Look for't; though it come late, it will come sure.

The punishment threatened is no less than damnation.

FRIAR: The more I hear, I pity thee the more;
   That one so excellent should give those parts
   All to a second death . . .

                        (v. 5.)

As has already been suggested, in '*Tis Pity She's a Whore*
Ford presents a world which his audience is invited to accept
as without reason. When the Friar preaches to Giovanni:

            Better to bless the sun
         Than reason why it shines

his words not only echo the doctrines of medieval Christianity
but foreshadow the demands made in Kafka's twentieth century world on the land-surveyor, K., by the powers above in
The Castle.† Giovanni challenges the might of those powers

---

   * *Jacobean Tragedy*, Methuen, 1962.
   † Franz Kafka, *The Castle*, 1927; v. p. 153.

by the most outrageous breach of the accepted law which Ford can imagine, the act of incest. In *The Castle* Amalia reverses the process and challenges them by obedience to a similar taboo: she refuses the obscene advances of one of the Castle's representatives. In both play and novel we are invited to jettison all previously conceived notions of good and evil as irrelevant to the demands of the forces which control our lives and whose demands are not understood unless, maybe, after they have been obeyed. Kafka presents Amalia as either a martyr or a criminal because she acts on her own conception of righteousness, exactly as Ford's hero also does. As a result of her action Amalia and her family become outcasts living in the utmost wretchedness and squalor, and Amalia herself lives like a saint, tending the parents whom her own action has brought to ruin. In this we at first see nothing but the exposure of the powers by the simple human capacity for loving-kindness. It is however necessary to remember Lear, exposed to the storm for his own redemption, as well as all the souls who pass through their Purgatories as best they may to find salvation at last. Perhaps closer to Kafka's situation may be that of *Measure for Measure*, where by lies and deception the duke achieves the moment in which Isabella kneels to plead for her enemy's life and finds blessing in her humility. At all events both Kafka and Ford feel only compassion for their enigmatic characters and leave judgement on their actions unpassed, and the gods that permit or cause their ruin, unjustified.

Giovanni's death does not make its impact on the mind as a punishment proper in itself, although meted out by men more evil than himself. His slaughterers are not devils carrying out the vengeance of a just God; his death is as unacceptable to human reason as that of Joseph K.* whose execution before his trial has properly begun, is as horrible as that of Ford's hero.

K. now perceived clearly that he was supposed to seize the knife himself, and plunge it into his own breast. But he did not do so, he merely turned his head which was still free to move, and gazed around him. . . . Where was the Judge whom he had never seen? Where was the High Court, to which he had never penetrated? He raised his hands and spread out all his fingers.

But the hands of one of the partners were already at K's. throat, while the other thrust the knife into his heart and turned it there twice. . . . 'Like a dog!' he said: it was as if he meant the shame of it to outlive him. (pp. 250–1)

Thus Ford, while retaining vestiges of the revenge convention of his day, apparently found that its material did not in itself mirror those elements of the human situation which were his primary concern. The achievement of justice is no longer meaningful to him. Like Chapman, he is more intent to suggest the value inherent in personal relationships and he shows them consummated only in death. In spite of the difference between Chapman's robust, virile rhythms and Ford's delicate, elusive melodies, the attitudes of the two men are nearer than might at first sight be supposed. Their heroes tend to be men outcast from or on the fringe of their respective societies, and the love of Clermont for Guise is almost as far removed from the accepted pattern as Giovanni's for Annabella. Both men appear to be retreating from the pressures of a society whose values they reject and attempting to contract out into private worlds where man is his own judge, and the writs of a commonly recognised law no longer run.

After Ford English society was to experience the fanaticism of the Puritan revolution, the detachment of the Augustan calm, the excitements of Romantic idealism, but across them all the twentieth century can hear such a voice and recognise in it an expression of its own dilemmas. We face again the disintegration of values, the violence and despair of our ancestors, as we strive to come to terms with the tensions of our own society in the activities of our own theatre.

F

Part II

THE MYTH OF THE WARRING BROTHERS IN THE CONTEMPORARY THEATRE

> Ass-Face drank
> The asses' milk of the stars . . .
> And the beavers building Babel
> Beneath each tree's thin beard,
> Said, 'Is it Cain and Abel
> Fighting again we heard?'
> It is Ass-Face, Ass-Face,
> Drunk on the milk of the stars,
> Who will spoil their horses of White lace—
> Expelled from the golden bars.
>
> Edith Sitwell, 'Ass-Face'

> Vision is a representation of what Eternally exists, Really and Unchangeably . . . the Hebrew Bible and the Gospel of Jesus are not Allegory but Eternal Vision or Imagination of all that exists . . . the writings of the prophets illustrate their conceptions of the Visionary Fancy by their various sublime and Divine Images as seen in the Worlds of Vision.
>
> William Blake, *A Vision of Judgment*

> To deny the myths and their dominion would be disastrous. To attempt to escape them by charging them with error —whether theological or rational—is an illusory enterprise. The point is to understand and feel their power.
>
> Denis de Rougemont, *The Myths of Love*

CHAPTER 3

HENRIK IBSEN
The Sinner his own Avenger

Your own self is your own Cain that murders your own
Abel. For every motion and notion of self has the spirit of
Anti-Christ and murders the spirit of God within you.

WILLIAM LAW

i. INTRODUCTION

As an introduction to a survey of the myth of the warring
brothers in the contemporary theatre, it may be of interest to
note that controversy concerning the viability of myth in a
scientific epoch has recently become explicit in the field of
religious thought in a form that reflects valuable light onto the
techniques of drama as well as onto those of theology. Perhaps
the most forthright attack on the use of symbol in the thinking of modern man is that of Rudolf Bultmann. Writing in
1950 Bultmann declares that to 'expect modern man to accept
the mythical view of the world as true . . . would be both
senseless and impossible . . . because . . . the mythical view
. . . is simply the cosmogony of a pre-scientific age'.* Later he
considers what he calls man's 'primitive notions of guilt and
punishment' and continues:

Gnostic influence suggests that . . . his (Christ's) death and
resurrection were . . . a cosmic event in which we were all involved.
It is only with an effort that modern man can think himself back
into such an intellectual atmosphere.†

Bultmann accordingly sets himself to 'demythologise' Christianity, rather as the naturalists once set themselves to 'de-

* Translated in *Kerygma and Myth*, ed. H. W. Bartsch, S.P.C.K., 1953,
vol. I, p. 3.   † Ibid., p. 8.

poetise' the drama, and his view of the intellectual processes of modern men led to a controversy which is as relevant to poetry as to religion. The following definition of Biblical myth, for example, could be applied almost unchanged to the material of the *Oresteia*, *King Lear* or–as will, it is hoped, be shown–to *Brand* and to the poetic drama of our own day. 'Myth . . . is one of the supreme creations of the human spirit. It is the narration of a heavenly process, presented in a definite, logical series of motifs reflected symbolically in objective events.'* J. J. Bachofen writes:

> The symbol (i.e. mythological symbolism) awakens intuition where the language of abstraction can only offer rational explanation. The symbol addresses every side of the human spirit, whereas the language of abstraction is bound to confine itself to a single thought . . . *Only the symbol can combine a wide variety of notions into a single total impression.*† (Italics the author's.)

The last sentence sums up admirably the end achieved by every successful poem, whether epic or dramatic.

Henrik Ibsen, the herald of the dramatic renaissance of the nineteenth century, was acclaimed and venerated as the apostle of naturalism with its passionate pretensions to scientific accuracy. In reality his work is that of a poet concerned with universal ideas, presented indeed by means of 'divine particulars', but never tied to the specific details of time and place demanded by a photographic realism.

Karl Jaspers, who seeks to reply to Bultmann as philosopher rather than as theologian, voices modern man's need for symbol–which the poets have indeed never neglected–in words which serve well as an introduction to the second part of this study.

Mythological thinking is not a thing of the past but characterises man in any epoch.

(a) The myth tells a story and expresses intuitive insights rather

---

* Alfred Jeremias, quoted ibid., p. 160.   † Ibid., p. 159.

than universal concepts . . . It is not a general idea, which can be
better and more directly grasped intellectually . . .

(b) The myth is carrier of meanings which can be expressed only
in the language of myth. They . . . are irreplaceable and unique.
They . . . are interpreted only by new myths, by being transformed.
Myths interpret each other.*

That myths do indeed interpret each other can be shown by
comparing the varied symbols used by an individual dramatist
and also by following the various forms of similar symbols in
the work of different writers. This belief informs the study
which follows.

ii. CAIN'S SIN INTERPRETED BY IBSEN

In the great renaissance of serious drama in the nineteenth
century, the violence which elicits the primal curse is shown at
first as heterosexual rather than homosexual in its nature, but
under many guises the sin which brings both guilt and punishment is still the same: Cain's sin—the closely-related individual
who should be especially cherished is the one who is made to
perish. The penalty is also the penalty of Cain: alienation from
the familiar world, ostracism, and, at last, destruction. In the
secular society of the modern world the suffering of Cain is not
less but greater than that imposed in the ordered universe
imagined by an earlier age. Camus writes:

> He who clings to a law does not fear the judgment that puts him
> in his place within an order he believes in. But the keenest of
> human torments is to be judged without law. Yet we die in that
> torment. God is not needed to create guilt or to punish. Our fellow-
> men suffice, aided by ourselves.†

As Webster with death, so Ibsen, it might be said, was
'much concerned with guilt'. This concern saturates his early
verse dramas *Brand* and *Peer Gynt*; it underlies the social
problems treated in the plays of his middle period, and it
becomes central once more in the last group of plays, begin-

* Alfred Jeremias, vol. II, p. 144.   † *The Fall*, Hamish Hamilton, 1957.

ning with *Rosmersholm* and ending with *When We Dead Awaken*. In his plays, however, the victim is always a woman. He has therefore discarded the Genesis version of the primordial murder for a possibly still older one.* The fact that a woman is sacrificed links the death more obviously to the theme of fertility, and it will in fact be seen that in every case it is his failure in a sexual relationship which is the hero's 'sin'. This is particularly clear in the last plays. John Rosmer could not accept Beata's passion, and Rebecca dared not offer him physical love. Alfred Allmers did indeed respond to Rita but resented his acquiescence and retreated from her demands. Solness failed with Aline, Borkman with Gunhild, whom he married, as he did with Ella whom he deserted; Rubek failed with Irene. On the other hand Rosmer accepted from Rebecca, as did Allmers from Asta, a love which made no physical demands and to which each man felt his response to be adequate. What did Solness demand of Hilde? What he offered her was a 'castle in the air'. In the earlier plays Peer denied Solveig as Brand, in another way, denied Agnes. Peer does indeed rejoice in his own sexuality, but he indulges it superficially, refusing any genuine commitment. Only late in her widowhood does Mrs. Alving understand and condemn her own frigidity and admit its tragic results. The same flaw in Hedda Gabler's nature drives her to voyeurism and suicide. Among the men Brand, Solness, Borkman and Rubek compensate for failure in personal relationships by creative work, and Rosmer and Allmers implicitly reveal their sexual inversion. All these men refuse the basic demands of woman and with them the demands of the child and therefore of life itself. Their violation of love paralyses the power to love and at last the power to live. Their death may be preceded by a wavering measure of awareness which admits a degree of self-judgement, but the 'Cain' may successfully defend himself against all conscious knowledge of his sin. In either case Ibsen is following patterns established in the thought and drama of the sixteenth and seventeenth centuries: that is to say he still

* cf. supra, pp. 12–13.

presents a moral world in which an absolute demand is
admitted and may be either accepted or refused. This is still
the world of Faustus and Othello, who admit their guilt and
accept their damnation, and of Macbeth and Ferdinand of
Arrogon who pay the penalty of their actions although denying
their responsibility.

iii. BRAND AND PEER GYNT

A study of Ibsen's dramatisations of the sin of murder and its
punishment may well begin with the two poetic dramas which
first brought him fame: *Brand* 1866 and *Peer Gynt* 1867.
Brand's murder is twofold: he causes the death of both his
wife and his child. Beneath his actions there lies a basic
dilemma, for Brand desires righteousness and sincerely believes he is acting righteously. Speaking of the hope of mankind he says:

> . . . it is The Will,
> the will to become God's creature again.
> For it is His Will that we regain
> The primal Adam, who was in His sight
> The tablet whereon He should write
> The characters of Heaven.*   (p. 29)

This appears to be Ibsen's version of Kierkegaard's demand
for a complete surrender of the will,† but men seem to be incapable of willing with consistency to become again the primal
Adam. They refuse the challenge that nothing less than complete surrender to what can be perceived of the purposes of
God is acceptable to Him. For better or worse they refuse the
demand of All or Nothing, and at the end of his life Brand
recognises his own failure as well as that of others.

The play's structure is a series of demands, all interpreted by

---

* All quotations from *Brand* are from the translation by James Forsyth,
Heinemann, 1960.

† e.g. in *Fear and Trembling* (v. infra, pp. 92, 149) Kierkegaard refers in
detail to the story of Abraham and Isaac which is prominent also in the
imagery of *Brand*.

Brand as the demands of God, which are in turn refused or accepted by those of whom they are made. The most important reactions, apart from Brand's own, are the contrasted ones of his mother and of his wife. Brand's description of his mother stealing the savings of her dead husband introduces for the first time in his work a symbol which persists into his last plays: the image of the burden on the back. Here the burden is merely compared to a carcass; for Rosmer it becomes the carcass itself.

> She swooped on her prey
> again and again till the bundles fell
> like carcasses. Then, like a lost soul
> inheriting the burden on its back,
> she slunk from the room.*

(p. 26)

This woman refuses her son's challenge to give up all her wealth in her search for salvation; she offers only 'almost all', and her son refuses her absolution before her death.

> The bread and wine of mercy require a clean table.

(p. 38)

By Agnes the demand for absolute consistency is in the end accepted.

The ultimate sacrifice for her is that of her child, whose life can only be preserved if her husband abandons his ministry in the northern mountains and takes his family to a softer climate. Echoing the story of Abraham, Agnes presents her son to God.

AGNES: (*raising the child in her arms*)
> God!—If such a sacrifice of life
> *is* your demand, then under your knife
> I dare thrust my own son!

(p. 49)

* A more literal translation by F. E. Garrett, Dent, 1915, runs: 'Like a damned soul she left the room *Happed up her find*' (p. 61).

For Brand the ultimate sacrifice is that of Agnes herself. When he exhorts and finally inspires her to give up her last earthly tie—even the grief she cherishes for the child she has lost—she warns him what the result will be.

AGNES: Your way is too narrow—too steep for me.

BRAND: For the Will there is no other way.

AGNES: And what of the way of Mercy?

BRAND: It is paved with the stones of sacrifice.
   First the Will, to pave the way
   toward that mercy—toward that day
   when his blinding light shall shine on you,
   and you shall see God's face.

AGNES: His face! . . .
   Who sees the face of God shall die!

   (p. 59)

Brand acts on his supposition that consistency in a course divinely appointed must be the divine Will, and he allows Agnes to die. He receives the answer to his anguish, if he does receive it, only in death, the cold death in the snow which is also the fate of those later murderers of love, Borkman and Rubek.*

BRAND: Here—in this white nothingness of death!—
   answer me God!—Is there hope above, for one
   who with his dying breath willed *all?*

The great shadow of the avalanche is closing over them as a Voice cries out of the tumult:

   God is love.

   (p. 98)

Whether Brand's death in the frozen waters of the snow-fall is redemption or destruction Ibsen leaves as doubtful as he does

* *John Gabriel Borkman* 1896; *When We Dead Awaken* 1899.

the fate of Peer Gynt. Certainly Brand's followers desert him
and stone him up the mountain-side, and the mad Gerd identifies him with the suffering Saviour:

> Please may I look at your hands? . . .
> Ah the print of the nails. . . .
> Blood!
> The blood to save us all—look,
> is going to waste staining the snow.   (pp. 94–5)

But the play, as a whole, does not enforce this identification.
Brand's dilemma is the same which Kierkegaard analyses in
Fear and Trembling. Here the myth of Abraham and Isaac
is used to present the situation of a man faced by the irrecon-
cilable demands of ethical judgement and religious faith. It
appears to be both right and wrong that Abraham should
sacrifice Isaac on the command of God. Kierkegaard finally
maintains that in every particular case faith in God must over-
leap any ethical principle which is, by definition, the result of
an intellectual generalisation. To the religious man Abraham's
course is plain; his dilemma is illusory. Ibsen never makes
Kierkegaard's leap, but it may well be the influence of Kierkegaard which makes *Brand*, in spite of the stark simplicity of its
outline, an ambiguous play. For all the obvious sympathy
with which his creator regards him, and in spite of Gerd's
final words, the authenticity of Brand's demands is never
established. Probably at the core of the play is the belief that
men can respond to no absolute demand because they are incapable of truly perceiving one. The incompatibility, to human
insight, of God's Justice and His Mercy, which had so fascinated
the medieval mind, had held the stage in the French *mystères* *
and more simply in the English *Parliament of Heaven*† and
the *Castle of Perseverance*.‡ At that time the seemingly
endless 'débat' could be resolved by an act of faith in God's

---

* e.g. *Mistère du Viel Testament*, Firmin Didot, 1878.
† *Ludus Coventriae*, E.E.T.S., Ex. Series, LXII.
‡ *Macro Moralities*, E.E.T.S., Ex. Series XCI.

transcendent Mercy (*Castle of Perseverance*) or by the inter-
position of the divine Son (*Parliament of Heaven*). This God of
Catholic medievalism had, however, been explicitly denied by
Brand, who derides what he holds to be the traditional God of
Christianity in his words to the painter, Einar:

> And what is the picture you have of your God? He's
> *old* isn't he? . . .
> And naturally—with age—he is—er—thin on top?—
> might have a hoary wisp of a beard;
> though kind, weird enough to get children scared
> into going to bed after tea;
> wears bedroom slippers—or should—shouldn't he? . . .
> Calm, Einer! I'm not mocking you.
> But isn't the God in most men's minds
> just such a figure? . . . .
> My God's a storm
> Yours a sighing in the wind.
> Mine is all love!—yours only kind.
>
> (p. 8)

Unlike Kierkegaard, Ibsen poses the dilemma in the terms of
the finite human judgement facing alternative absolute values.
In these terms it is inapprehensible and unanswerable. The
question implicit in Brand's words and actions is therefore
'meaningless'.

Peer Gynt accepts the Troll king's dictum: 'To thyself be
enough.' He does not, however, apply it consistently. He
leaves Solveig because he is not prepared to make the sacrifices
which joining his life to hers would involve, but he asks her to
wait for him, and he cannot forget her. His guilt is summed up
in his surrender to the Boyg—defined as: 'a goblin snake coiled
up round a man; a mythical representation of a man's sinful
past'.* Peer fought the Boyg in the mountains and temporarily
escaped from him, but his dictum: 'Go round about, Peer',
proved irresistible, because it was a temptation to the sin which
was already habitual, the tradition Peer had already estab-

* Brynildren, *Norwegian Dictionary*.

lished for himself by his own conduct. The structure of *Peer Gynt*, like that of *Brand*, is serial. The first part consists of the sequence of evasions by which Peer escapes from the demands of the family, of society and of sexual love. The climax of this sequence comes when Peer faces the challenge of his mother's death-bed. In this case he can no longer be blinded by the appearance of success which had so often given a temporary gloss to the issue of his earlier adventures. The contrast between Peer and Brand is always clear in general terms, but Ibsen enforces it when he designs the manner in which each man faces the crisis of his mother's death. Brand's only concern is that his mother should recognise the price necessary for salvation, face the reality of her situation and act in accordance with it.

> When you repent I'll come.
> But *I* must make one condition too. . . .
> That all that binds you to the earth—
> All monies and goods you must. . . .
> > . . . *renounce.*
> And go down naked as at birth
> To the grave's encounter. . . . (p. 28)
>
> Then, Mother, I'll sing
> Songs by your bed, whose love will ring
> Joyous echoes from these rocks. (p. 27)

Peer does sing songs to his mother, and they are songs of love for her, but his purpose is the reverse of Brand's, and it succeeds only too well.*

PEER: Wrap yourself up in the bed-clothes.
   I'll sit on the end of the bed,
   And we'll while away the evening.
   I'll sing as you once sang to me, ...
AASE: Please, Peer, will you bring me my prayer-book?
   I'm uneasy in my mind.

* All quotations from *Peer Gynt* are from the translation by Norman Ginsbury, Hammond and Hammond, 1946.

PEER: In Soria Moria castle,
  King and Prince are giving a feast.
  Now lie back on your pillow,
  I'm going to drive you there.   (p. 71)

As the fairy story is built up Aase surrenders completely to the
fascination of its unreality and dies in her illusion.

PEER: Gee-up! Look alive there, Blackie! . . .

AASE: Are you sure you're on the right road?

PEER: (*cracking whip again*)
  It's an easy road to follow. . . .

AASE: I'll lie back and close my eyes now
  And trust to you, my own boy.
                                                  (p. 71)

Neither Brand nor Peer therefore succeeds in saving the
mother he loves, but Brand's mother's dying words are a pre-
echo of the last words of the play; they are therefore significant although as ambiguous as the ending itself. They convey the suggestion that in spite of her greed and her com-
promises she still approached the truth more nearly than did
the ruthlessly consistent priest.

  God has not so hard a fist as my son.
                                                  (p. 43)

Aase, dying in the arms of the son whom she had cherished
with such real, albeit such foolish, devotion, may similarly be
nearer the Kingdom of Heaven than she knew.

  The falsity of Peer's basic assumption 'To thyself be enough'
is revealed in the high point of the middle section of the play,
when he visits a Cairo lunatic asylum. Here the inmates live
each one in the world of his own subjective vision and is
therefore actually 'enough' to himself.

BEGRIFFENFELDT: Here, we're ourselves from the very word 'go'

We're ourselves and nothing but ourselves.
We speed full sail ahead as ourselves,
We shut ourselves up in a keg of self,
We stew in our own juice, we seal ourselves up
Hermetically with a bung of self. . . .
There are no thoughts or sorrows outside our own;
We are ourselves in thought and in word,
Ourselves to the farthest, the uttermost edge.   (p. 118)

Among the lunatics is a fellah who, in his private world, is
King Apis. He carries his illusion on his back in the form of a
mummy of the late king who he now believes himself to be,
and this is therefore a visual symbol of the dead past which
cannot be buried but must be continually carried forward with
guilt and misery.*

FELLAH: Do you see this thing on my back?
    He was once a king called Apis;
    Today he is known as a mummy;
    In addition, he is dead. . . .
    Now give me some sound advice, will you? . . .
    How can I become like King Apis
    And confound those who think I'm a fake?

Peer, forgetting the consistency current in this utterly self-
contained world, suggests that the man hang himself:

                    and then
        In your coffin, in the earth's bosom,
        You'll behave as though you were dead.
                                    (pp. 121–2)

His jocular advice is accepted in earnest, and when another
man, believing he is a pen, sharpens himself by cutting his
throat Peer realises for a moment the horror of the isolated,
uncommitted life.

* This interpretation does not, of course, exclude one more generally
accepted, i.e. that 'King Apis' represents the Swedish nation. Political and
psychological material are both present; we are here concerned with the
latter.

What shall I–? What am I? Great God–hold fast! . . .
Help me, Thou! Oh, Protector of Madmen, help!

He is forced to recognise, though only fleetingly, his kinship
with these people; as he sinks to the ground, Begriffenfeldt,
with a crown of straw in his hand, makes a spring and seats
himself athwart Peer.

BEGRIFFENFELDT: Ha! Look at him, sitting enthroned in the
    mire!
  He's beside himself! We'll crown him there!
  Long live the Emperor, the Emperor of Self.

(p. 124)

In the third and final section of the play Peer at last
glimpses the sin for which he is to be destroyed. He knows
himself as the onion, which, when he has peeled it, shows itself
to be without a core. As he wanders through the forest thread-
balls catch at his feet, and their voices speak from the ground:

> We are thoughts;
> You should have thought us!
> Legs to move on,
> You should have brought us!

The leaves fly past whispering:

> We are passwords;
> You should have known us!

From the air comes the sigh:

> We are the songs
> You have left unsung!

The dewdrops fall from the trees:

> We are tears
> That would never fall!

G

Broken straws make the final accusation:

> We are deeds
> You have left undone! . . .
> On the Day of Judgment
> We shall be there
> To tell our story
> And then, beware!*

(pp. 147–9)

For this was Solveig left alone in the hut in the forest.

The men in the last plays refuse and destroy the women who love them, but at least they experience some conflict between the claims of the world of artistic or social achievement and the world of personal relationships, and recognise that it is the acceptance of one system of values which destroys another. Peer has met the claim of neither world. From the Button-Moulder's threat that he be melted down he at last attempts to seek shelter with Solveig, a bankrupt in terms of both.

> 'Round about,' said the Boyg.
>   No! No! This time
> It's straight through no matter how narrow the path!
> Pass judgment on the sinner before you! . . .
>   Cry my sins aloud.

Solveig refuses to pass judgement:

> You have made my life a beautiful song.
> Bless you for having come back at last!   (pp. 168–9)

The play ends with her defiance of the Button-Moulder as her song grows louder in order to drown his threat of the meeting at the last cross-roads.

* Compare this with the existentialist *mauvaise foi* of Electra, p. 138, and Von Gerlach, p. 145.

I will rock you and watch beside you.
Sleep and dream, my own dear love.   (p. 170)

What then did Ibsen intend to be the significance of his
conclusion? Peer first met Solveig in the naturalistic setting of
Ingrid's wedding-party, and there is no suggestion at that
point that she is either more or less 'real' than Peer himself,
Mad Moens or Aslak the smith. When Peer meets her in the
forest the dramatic convention has shifted. Peer, who has been
made an outlaw and is facing exile and loneliness, is building a
hut.

PEER: I must fix a bolt, a bolt to keep out
    The venomous breed of hobgoblins.
    They come when night falls; they knock and they rap,
    'Open, Peer Gynt, we're as nimble as thoughts.'

                                                     (pp. 61-2)

As he works he hears Solveig's voice and then sees her coming
towards him. The apparition is doubtless 'real' enough to be
either Peer's salvation or his undoing, but does it exist in the
dreamer's mind or in the world around him? The other
dramatic characters in the scene are the Troll princess and the
crooked child born of her as a result of Peer's 'thoughts and
desires'.

WOMAN: If you want to see me as fair as before,
    You need only show that girl there the door,
    Put her out of your mind and out of your sight; . . .
    When you're sitting in the fireside glow
    And you want to love her and kiss and embrace,
    I'll be at your side in my rightful place.
    We'll share you. We'll take it in turns in your bed.
    Farewell, my dear Peer, now go and get wed.   (p. 65)

No words in the play ring truer than Peer's conclusion.

        We were so near; and now she's walled in.
        And beauty and joy have departed for ever.

> Go round about. There is no way
> Straight through from me to her. (p. 66)

If Solveig is presented here as a memory and a wish within Peer's mind, so that her figure and that of the Troll woman externalise the conflict between the two ways of loving of each of which Peer knows only 'enough', then Solveig of the last scene also may possess this the same kind of being. Salvation by a return to the mother's womb is a salvation desired by many, but Ibsen is unlikely to attribute objective reality to fantasies bred of such a desire, or to suggest that a human Solveig could answer Peer's impossible demands, any more than Torvald Helmer could satisfy Nora's or that the building of an orphanage could assuage Mrs. Alving's puzzled remorse. Peer by his desertion destroys the girl Solveig; the song he hears in his old age is no more but also no less than the work of his own imagination. He knew the value of the truth which in his acts he had denied.

> The boy shall lie against his mother's heart
> The whole day long. He is weary now
> Sleep my dear; my precious one, sleep, sleep.
> I will rock you my boy, my darling, sleep, sleep.
> (p. 170)

With his destruction of Solveig Peer destroyed also the self that might have loved her, and therefore the Button-Moulder awaits him at the third cross-roads to melt him down in the casting ladle of oblivion.

iv. THE LAST PLAYS*

(a) Rosmersholm

It has already been suggested that *Rosmersholm* affords a bridge between the drama which presents the concept of

---

* References in this section are to the translations by Una Ellis-Fermor (*The Master Builder and Other Plays*, published Penguin, 1958) except in the case of *When We Dead Awaken* where the translation used is that by M. Myers, Hart-Davis, 1960.

justice in an era of religious faith and that which presents it in
an era of scepticism.* In the world of this play the moral law
of a Christian society survives as an absolute value relevant to
two distinct situations. The agnostic, John Rosmer, accepts it in
relation to marriage and in relation to murder. Rebecca West,
on the other hand, holds to values which over-ride such a law.
She gives priority to personal freedom and personal love. She
believes that she was choosing freely between two valid
imperatives, and chose to obey the higher when she sought to
bring about Beata's death so that she might marry John. As a
result of her passion, however, she abandoned her own faith
and espoused his. That is to say she accepted guilt for the sin of
murder irrespective of motive, and accepted also the righteousness of punishment according to the Mosaic law of a life for a
life. John also accepts responsibility for Beata's suicide, but
Ibsen makes it plain that his overwhelming sense of guilt
springs from a deeper root. Long before Rebecca arrived on the
scene, and, as she expressed it, 'took action', John was himself
destroying his wife by his inability to respond to her passionate love.

JOHN: *(to Kroll)*
I've told you about that uncontrollable fierce passion of hers–that
she insisted I should meet. Oh the horror she filled me with.
                                                        (p. 60)

Rebecca also felt passionate love for John, but realising he
could never respond to it, she mastered it and offered him a
different sort of love–one which he was able to accept.

REBECCA: There came over me . . . this wild uncontrolled passion . . . oh John.

JOHN: Passion? You–! For what?

REBECCA: For you . . . It came over me like a storm at sea. It was
like one of those storms we can get up North in winter. . . . But

* v. supra, p. 22.

when I came to live with you here, in stillness, in solitude, when you told me all your thoughts without reserve, every mood you felt however tender and exquisite, then . . . this ugly passion . . . went away from me . . . Peace of mind came down over me—like the stillness on the mountain cliffs at home under the midnight sun.

JOHN: Tell me some more about it. Everything you can describe.

REBECCA: There isn't much more, my dear. Only this, that then love began in me. The great selfless love that is content with sharing life in the way we have done.   (pp. 107–9)

But although Rebecca believes she is able to offer John what he needs, she knows that what she offers is incomplete.

REBECCA: the Rosmer view of life does ennoble. But—but—but—

JOHN: But? Well?

REBECCA: —but it kills joy, my dear.   (p. 109)

The love which John offers Rebecca is the love that, in *Little Eyolf*, Allmers enjoys with the boy-girl, Asta, but Asta, though less experienced, is wiser than Rebecca. In her Ibsen creates a character who knows that such an incomplete love means destruction, and who has the strength to refuse it.

The self-inflicted punishment of John and Rebecca is their double suicide, but the motive transcends the desire for expiation. Rebecca dies ostensibly because she caused the death of Beata:

Where I have sinned, it is right I should expiate.

(p. 117)

The driving force however is the positive belief that her death will enfranchise her lover:

REBECCA: But suppose I did have the courage? And the glad will? What then?

JOHN: . . . Then I should have faith again . . . in my power to
ennoble men's minds. (p. 116)

He shares the sense of guilt for Beata which he believes it
meet should be expiated but which he has carried, admitted
but unpurged, in spite of his protestation to Rebecca:

I won't go through life with a corpse on my back.
(p. 78)

Beyond this he feels himself guilty of apostasy to his Christian
faith and to the society into which he was born. But deeper than
all these more or less conscious motives is the unrealised fact
that he cannot face life alone; if Rebecca dies—as he believes
she should—he must die with her. Hence he goes through a
symbol of marriage with her and then claims: 'Man and wife
should go together.'

What, if not expiation for their sins, does the death of these
two in the mill-race achieve? For John, this last apparently
fatal choice, marks the first time he has been able to commit
himself to decisive action. He had evaded the demands of his
marriage as he had those of his change of faith. Like Peer
Gynt, he had listened only too readily to the advice of the
Boyg: Go round about. It is the first thing that Ibsen tells
about him. Rebecca and the housekeeper are watching him
approach the house.

MRS. HELSETH: Is he going to take the foot-bridge? . . .

REBECCA: No. He's turning off. Going up and round again today.
All that way round.

MRS. HELSETH: . . . Of course it must come hard for the master
to cross that bridge. A place where a thing like that's happened.
(p. 30)

It is this new power of commitment which is significant, for
in spite of the fact that it is Beata's death which precipitates
their own, John and Rebecca do not finally die for punishment; they die for love.

The acceptance of their destiny comes slowly at first.

JOHN: People don't lend themselves to ennobling from without, you know.

REBECCA: Not through tranquil love, do you think?

JOHN: Yes, *that* of course would be the great thing.   (p. 110)

Rebecca recognises that, for John, such a love is the only alternative to a morality of prohibitions which ensures a guilt destructive of faith in the self and finally in life.

REBECCA: Oh this murdering doubt! John—John! . . .

JOHN: I don't believe in myself in any way any more. I don't believe in myself or in you . . . I don't see that I *can* live it out . . . I can't bear this desolation—this terrible emptiness.   (p. 111)

At the beginning of the play, that is two days before her death, Rebecca has nearly finished the knitting of a large white shawl the last stitches of which are made during the hours in which she watches her hopes ripen towards fulfilment only to fall unfulfilled. This white shawl she picks up and slowly puts over her head when she promises John to win back his faith by throwing herself into the mill-race. Here she is putting on the white robe of a penitent which is also her shroud. But there is another sacrament to which a woman goes in white, and the union that takes place on the mill bridge may be a true marriage consummated at last.

JOHN: The husband must go with the wife, as the wife with the husband.

REBECCA: Yes, but tell me this first. Is it you that go with me, or I that go with you?

JOHN: We two go with each other, Rebecca. I with you and you with me.

REBECCA: I almost believe that too.

JOHN: For now we two are *one*.   (p. 118)

But the hands of time can be turned still further backward so that Rebecca's shawl becomes also her christening robe, for the waters of the mill-race are not only those of death but also those of baptism. Since the neophyte rises from such waters to the fullness of a new life, the symbol of the punishment for the murder of love becomes identified with the symbol of rebirth into a world where love is triumphantly fulfilled at last. It is not often that Ibsen is able to make such a positive statement, and even here an ambiguity obtrudes itself. Rebecca's acceptance of the glory in her tragic 'marriage' is easily credible, but what of Rosmer? The 'white horses' of a death-bearing tradition had ranged round his home from his boyhood. Have we in him, disguised even from himself, the self-appointed avenger of the earlier drama, and if so is he presented to us as a righteous or as an evil justicer? Ibsen leaves no doubt that he dies self-deceived, the slave of a code for which he is able to bring forward no better justification than that it is a framework within which he finds the security to judge – and condemn – his own acts. Perhaps, however, Ibsen intends to show that he achieves freedom in love at the very last moment of his life. Mrs. Helseth, watching from the window through which she and Rebecca have seen him avoid the bridge two days earlier, now cries out:

That white thing there–! they're both standing on the footbridge. God forgive the sinful creatures! If they're not putting their arms round each other. Ah! Over the bridge–both of them! Out into the mill-race.

Rebecca died to give her lover the power to live, and in fact gave him the strength to die – whether for love or for justice's sake Ibsen leaves obscure; the cumulative effect of the imagery used here and in the following plays does, however, suggest the possible triumph of love in death. Whether or not Ibsen was aware of the full significance to the human mind of the imagery he used, must remain uncertain and is indeed irrelevant. Many a man has dug his foundations deeper and built his house better than he consciously perceived.

(b) The Master-Builder

When Hilde questions Halvard Solness concerning his fear of climbing the tower which he has built, her words are a direct accusation:

HILDE: But you're afraid of it—you are, aren't you?

SOLNESS: Yes, I am.

HILDE: Afraid you'll fall down and kill yourself?

SOLNESS: No, not that.

HILDE: What, then?

SOLNESS: I'm afraid of retribution, Hilde.   (p. 203)

Again the guilt with which Ibsen is concerned is the guilt of the killing of love. Solness fears retribution for the wrong he has done his wife, and the strength of his guilt is shown by the determination with which he usually refuses to consider it.

MRS. SOLNESS: You can build as much as ever you like, Halvard— you'll never manage to build a real home again for *me*!

SOLNESS: Well then, for heaven's sake don't let's talk about it any more.

MRS. SOLNESS: We never do talk about it, anyhow. Because you just put it away from you.   (p. 159)

He does however admit his guilt and fear to Hilde.

SOLNESS: Everything that I've succeeded in making, building, shaping into beauty . . . I've got to make good. Pay for it. Not in money. But with human happiness.

(p. 171)

I'll tell you what luck feels like. It feels like a great, raw place here on my breast. And the servers and ministers keep on flaying

pieces of skin off other people to mend *my* wound! But yet the
wound isn't healed. Never,—never!

(p. 177)

Solness' achievements as a master-builder began with the fire
which burned down his wife's old home and caused the deaths
of their children, and he believes that this means that they
sprang directly from the destruction of his wife as a human
being. In this he is in fact mistaken; with characteristic irony
Ibsen makes it plain that Aline Solness' life was not in fact
destroyed by the fire and its sequel. Even before she met her
husband she was abnormally retarded in her development:

MRS. SOLNESS: Oh no, no, Miss Wangel. Don't talk to me any
more about the two little boys . . . No, it's the small losses in life
that cut one to the heart . . . All the old portraits on the wall
were burnt. And so were all the old silk dresses . . . And then all
the dolls.

HILDE: The dolls?

MRS. SOLNESS: (*choking with sobs*) I had nine beautiful dolls . . .

HILDE: Why, had you kept all those dolls put away? Ever since you
were little?

MRS. SOLNESS: Not put away. The dolls and I had gone on living
together all the time.

HILDE: After you were married too?

MRS. SOLNESS: Oh yes. So long as he did not see it.

(p. 191)

Halvard's sin against his wife was thus a negative one. He had
not actually killed her power to love, only failed to awaken it.
Possibly his creator did not consider his responsibility any the
less. In any case he shows his hero carrying his dead past with
him as surely as did John Rosmer, who so passionately pro-
tested that he would not go on with a dead body tied to his
back.

SOLNESS: And now she's dead—for my sake. And I'm living,
chained to the dead.
(p. 194)

He himself cannot escape however, for his loveless life has thwarted his own power to love as well as Aline's. When Hilde comes with the challenge of her youthful sexuality he longs to respond, but no genuine mutuality in love is possible to him.

SOLNESS: Now I see it. Human beings haven't any use for these homes of theirs. Not for being happy in. And I shouldn't have had any use for a home like that either . . . Nothing, nothing—the whole thing, nothing! . . . The only thing I think human beings can be happy in—that's what I'll build now. . . . The castles in the air, yes. (p. 205)

Hilde defines such creations and their purpose when she says:

Castles in the air, they're so easy to hide in. And easy to build too. (pp. 197–8)

When Solness attempts in sober earnest to approach Hilde, first by suggesting their flight and finally by his ascent of the tower, he is destroyed.

The tower is not, however, solely a phallic symbol; it is also the heavenly throne, to which man can only aspire by arrogating to himself divinity. The sin of Halvard Solness neither began nor ended with the death-in-life to which, in the service of his own achievement, he condemned his wife. He had risen on the shoulders of the old man who had taught him his trade and whom he had kicked from beneath him when his usefulness was past, but he himself refused to accept the processes of time by which in his turn he would be displaced. When he exploits Kara and prevents the natural rise of Ragnar, he is denying the natural law of change in time, and in thus defying time he is defying the limitations of the human condition. As well as the sin of Cain he commits the sin of Lucifer, and his final fall from the tower unites in one symbolic movement the catastrophic culmination of both crimes. Solness knows well enough that in seeking permanence he is seeking the impossible, but his knowledge does not enable him to defend himself against his horror of what, by the law of kind, is inevitable.

SOLNESS: The luck will turn. I can feel it . . . Some day the younger generation will come knocking on my door.

DR. HERDAL: Well, good gracious, what about it?

SOLNESS: What about it? Why then it's all up with Solness the master-builder. . . . What's that? Did you hear anything?

DR. HERDAL: It's someone knocking.

SOLNESS: (*loudly*) Come in. (pp. 140–1)

There enters the Angel of Death in the guise of the beautiful maiden–dressed in a climbing skirt and carrying an Alpine-stock–the youthful Hilde whose demand for his love is to be the instrument of his destruction.

Solness himself specifically connects the play's twin themes of time and guilt:

SOLNESS: It's a very good thing you have come to me now.

HILDE: *Is* it good?

SOLNESS: . . . I'd begun to be afraid . . . The younger generation –its retribution you see. It comes in the forefront of the change.
(p. 154)

Solness has judged himself guilty, and his attempt to ignore his guilt and find the love he has forfeited is mortal to him. His death completes the circle started by his *hubris*; does it also fulfil his quest for love? In *Rosmersholm* Ibsen allows to John and Rebecca an ecstatic though fleeting consummation of passion in the moment of death, as he allows it also to Rubek and Irene at the end of *When We Dead Awaken*. To Halvard and Hilde such a rare felicity is denied. The woman does experience her moment of ecstasy, but she is alone. The validity of her triumph is denied by the facts; it is one of those 'castles in the air' of which she had already shown her understanding. Now she succumbs to their magic and builds one in which she may hide after her lover's death.

HILDE: I hear a song. A mighty song (*crying out in wild jubilation and joy*). Oh, let us send him up a greeting in return! For now, now it's done.

But Solness falls.

HILDE: I can't see him up there now.

RAGNAR: Terrible business, so he couldn't manage it.

HILDE: But he got right to the top. And I heard harps in the air. *My – my* master-builder.

Her illusion is as palpable as Peer Gynt's when he hears Solveig's song only in his imagination. Like Peer, Solness has sinned by going 'round about' to the end, and in the view of their creator, both men are fit only for the casting-ladle and the Oblivion for whom Time fills his wallet with just such inconsiderable alms.

(c) *Little Eyolf*

Alfred and Rita Allmers, although they both claim to be agnostics, both accept that the death of their little crippled son is a punishment for their own sensuality.

ALLMERS: (*flaring up suddenly*) You're the guilty one here! . . . Yes, *you*! . . . It was you who left that tiny child lying on the table to look after himself.

RITA: . . . you had promised to look after the child.

ALLMERS: Yes I had. But then you came . . .

RITA: Say rather that you forgot the child and everything else.

ALLMERS: (*in suppressed fury*) Yes, that's true . . . I forgot the child – in your arms. . . . We've sinned, both of us. And so there *was* retribution in Eyolf's death. . . . A judgment on you and me. . . . This thing that we're now calling grief and bereavement – it's the gnawing of conscience, Rita. Nothing else.

(pp. 257–8)

But below the neglect of his child lies another sin of destruction for which retribution will be exacted. Alfred Allmers, like John Rosmer and Halvard Solness, wrongs his wife by a loveless marriage undertaken for material advantage, and in all these plays Ibsen makes the fruits of such a marriage death— the death of a child or a wife or both. In *Little Eyolf* the double price is not in fact exacted, but the play's central situation is the same as that of its two immediate predecessors and its two successors.

ALLMERS: I did not share your passion from the first.

RITA: . . . how did I win you then? . . . It was 'the gold and green forests' as you call it, wasn't it, Alfred?

ALLMERS: Yes.

(p. 261)

Both partners feel the guilt of sexual inadequacy, of the failure to measure up to the basic demands of life which means in effect the service of death. Rita suffers because she is unable to win the love of the man she loves or even to hold him as a sexual partner. Allmers' guilt is more subtle. He refuses Rita's passion because he has been satisfied with a love which he believes was entirely asexual: the love of his half-sister, Asta, whom he had brought up and protected. In fact their relationship is highly erotic and has its roots in Allmers' latent homosexuality:

ALLMERS: And then, when we two were left alone in the world, we two. . . .

ASTA: That was a happy time for us, Alfred, when all's said. We two alone.

ALLMERS: Yes, it was. Hard as we worked . . . my dear, faithful Eyolf.

ASTA: Oh! you mustn't remind me of that stupid trick with the name. . . .

ALLMERS: You looked out the old clothes I'd had as a boy—

ASTA: Your best Sunday suit, yes. Can you remember the blue blouse and the shorts?

ALLMERS: (*with his eyes resting on her*) How well I remember you when you used to put them on and wear them.

ASTA: Yes, but I only did it when we were at home alone.

(p. 247)

In spite of the fact that in *Rosmersholm* a form of marriage, the symbol of a full heterosexual love, is retained, this love of Allmers and Asta resembles that which Rebecca schools herself to offer to Rosmer, and which he is at last able to accept. Clear as the Asta-Allmers relationship is made, however, Ibsen does not create a situation in which Allmers himself becomes conscious of his inversion and of guilt because of it. His conscious guilt is focused on his failure as husband and father; the root cause of this failure, however, is made sufficiently obvious.

Unlike Rosmer, Allmers retains no theological language in which to voice his distress, but he does retain the desire to find a pattern in existence such as had been expressed in the old religion.

ALLMERS: . . . there must be a meaning in it. Life, existence, destiny can't surely be so utterly meaningless.

ASTA: Oh Alfred, my dear, who can say anything for certain about these things?

ALLMERS: (*laughing bitterly*) No; you're probably right there. Perhaps the whole thing . . . goes its own way like a drifting wreck without a rudder.   (p. 244)

The play is unique among Ibsen's later works in that it attempts to express, in humanistic terms, a form of redemption in life rather than in death. Rita proposes to undertake the care of 'all those poor, outcast children', who, she believes, were in part responsible for the death of her own child. She says to her husband:

You have made an empty place in me. And I must try to fill it up with something. Something which could seem like love.

(p. 281)

Alfred agrees to join with her, and he has, as he always has, fine words with which to express his purpose:

Up,—to the mountain-tops. To the stars. And to the great stillness.

(p. 283)

But Rita is more realistic; she knows that although he is returning to her he will remember not only the child Eyolf, in whose name the work is to be undertaken, but also the 'big Eyolf', who has left him because she knew his dilemma would be insoluble if she remained. Yet the punishment of the destroyer may, it appears, be remitted, if the potential victim lives to offer forgiveness, and the sinner struggles towards emancipation from the past. The auguries are poor however. The play does not promise the triumphs of love achieved in their anguish by John and Rebecca, and the last words of the dialogue re-voice in different terms the terrible clutch of the past which Ibsen never allows us to forget. He does not use here the recurrent image of the body on the back, but the past remains to haunt the minds of those who would be safer if it were forgotten.

ALLMERS: And we shall know then, perhaps, that the spirits are with us . . . Yes. They will be beside us perhaps—those whom we have lost.

RITA: Our little Eyolf. And your big Eyolf, too.

ALLMERS: It may be that, once or twice on life's way, we shall see a glimpse of them.

(p. 282)

Ibsen did not endow Allmers with the kind of strength which made it likely that such visions would be either rare, or unde-structive of his too easily adopted resolutions for the future.

H

(d) *John Gabriel Borkman* and *When We Dead Awaken*

Ibsen's last two plays for the most part re-echo themes already heard. John Gabriel Borkman has the dead bodies of two women on his back—the one that of the woman whom he loved and deserted, the other that of the woman whom he did not love and married. The long dialogue between the self-immured bankrupt and his early love, Ella, makes the main point perhaps over-explicitly.

ELLA: Can it be true, what you said, that at that time I was the dearest thing in the world to you?

BORKMAN: Both then and after—long, long after.

ELLA: And yet you sold me, all the same . . . You are a murderer! You have committed the deadly sin!

BORKMAN: You're raving, Ella.

ELLA: You have killed the power to love in me. . . . The great, unpardonable sin—it's the sin of killing love in a human creature. . . . *That's* the double murder you made yourself guilty of. The murder of your own soul and of mine.

(pp. 330–2)

His wife's accusation is similar.

MRS. BORKMAN: You have never loved anything outside yourself—that's the core of the matter.

BORKMAN: I have loved power—

MRS. BORKMAN: You once had the power to make *me* happy. Did you use it for that?

BORKMAN: (*without looking at her*) Someone has to go down as a rule—in a ship-wreck. (p. 344)

Unlike all Ibsen's other 'Cains' Borkman deals successfully, from his own point of view, with his sense of guilt.

Time after time . . . I have been my own accuser, my own defence, and my own judge. . . . And the verdict I came back to every time is *this*, that the only person I have sinned against is myself. . . . To put it briefly, I have acquitted myself.

(pp. 342–3)

When, however, Borkman leaves the gallery where he has paced like a caged lion for eight long years, he finds his acquittal is valid only in his own mind, and the cold hostility of the outside world destroys him. Looking from the snow-covered clearing at the mountains in whose rocks he imagines the veins of the hidden riches which his projects never brought to the surface, he says to Ella:

> Do you see the mountain ranges, *there*, far away? One behind another. They rise up. They tower. *That* is my deep, unending, inexhaustible kingdom.

ELLA: Yes John, but there's a freezing breath coming from that kingdom! . . . you'll never win the reward you asked for murder. You will never march in triumph into your dark, cold kingdom.

(pp. 367–8)

Ella is right; Borkman dies in the snow, leaving behind him two lonely women, existing only as the ghosts he had made of them.

MRS. BORKMAN: We two twin sisters—over the man we both loved.

ELLA: We two shadows—over the dead man.

(p. 370)

The reward he gained for murder was, as he might well have foreseen, death.

Rubek, the sculptor in *When We Dead Awaken*, describes himself as he is represented in one of his own sculptures.

RUBEK: But listen how I have portrayed myself . . . beside a spring . . . there sits a man weighed down by guilt . . . I call him remorse—remorse for a forfeited life. He sits there dipping his fingers in the rippling water to wash them clean, and he is gnawed and tormented by the knowledge that he will never succeed. He will never . . . free himself and be granted resurrection. He must stay for ever in his Hell.

IRENE: Poet!

(p. 53)

The statue might serve as a portrait of John Rosmer, Halvard Solness, Alfred Allmers or J. G. Borkman, although they would none of them have had the self-knowledge necessary for its production. Rubek's sin was also the same as theirs. He destroyed love, and the woman in whom he destroyed it, his model Irene, returns as from the dead to accuse him. He meets her in a mountain resort where she is a mental patient.

RUBEK: Some string inside you has broken.

IRENE: Doesn't that always happen when someone dies?

RUBEK: Oh Irene, forget those wild ideas! You are alive! Alive, alive!

IRENE: I was dead for many years. They came and tied me up, tied my arms together behind my back. Then they lowered me into a tomb, with iron bars across the door, and padded walls so that no-one up above could hear the shrieks of the dead . . .

RUBEK: Do you blame me for this? Do you hold me guilty?

IRENE: Yes.   (p. 33)

But Rubek's sin was not only that he left Irene, but that he had exploited her and so treated another human being as a means to an end.

IRENE: And then you were finished with me . . . You had no further use for me . . . You killed my soul and then you model yourself as a figure of penance. And in your eyes that settles your account.   (pp. 35 and 54)

And in effect Rubek accepts this statement for he answers: 'I am an artist, Irene.' At the end of the play images from early works crowd in: Solness' tower, Brand's avalanche, Borkman's snowfield accompany another death in love like that of John and Rebecca.

RUBEK: Then let us two dead people live life to the full for one short hour before we go down again into our graves . . . Will you come with me now, my bride of grace? . . .

IRENE: Yes, through the mists. And then up to the top of our tower where it shines in the sunrise.

(. . . *Rubek and Irene, hand in hand, climb upwards towards the snowfield . . . Suddenly a roar like thunder is heard from high up on the snowfield which rushes down whirling . . .*)

THE NUN: Irene!
Pax Vobiscum.   (pp. 68–9)

John and Rebecca went knowingly to death. Brand was purposefully seeking God, but Rubek and Irene appear to have lost all touch with reality as man perceives it and expect to achieve their joy by living in the cold of the snowfield. Their illusion is as profound as John Gabriel Borkman's, their miscalculation as fatal as that of Halvard Solness. Like so many others, having sinned they move in blindness to their own undoing. If any non-rational intuition guides them to their redemption Ibsen makes no overt statement to that effect.

In all these plays Ibsen imagines the destroyer destroyed by his own past deed through the effects of his guilt on his own mind. In only one play does he draw a human being wise, resilient, and generous enough to forgive herself and so be able to continue the business of living and loving. The one character who seems able to cope successfully with a past which is considered to be sinful is Gina, the devoted wife of Hjalmar Ekdal, in *The Wild Duck*.* The conversation between her and her husband, after he has learned of her early liaison with her former employer, is a supreme example of the beauty of commonsense infused with love.

* *Hedda Gabler and Other Plays*, trans. Una Ellis-Fermor, Penguin Books, 1961.

GINA: Do you regret the fourteen-fifteen years we have lived together?

HJALMAR: Tell me. Haven't you—every hour, every day—regretted the web of deceit you've spun round me like a spider? Answer me! Haven't you really been going about in an agony of regret and remorse?

GINA: Oh, my dear Hjalmar, I've had so much to do, looking after the house and all the everyday jobs—

HJALMAR: So you never gave a thought to your past life?

GINA: No. God knows I'd nearly forgotten all that old business . . . But tell me, Hjalmar, what would have become of you if you hadn't had a wife like me?

HJALMAR: Like you! . . .

GINA: Oh, Hjalmar, you mustn't say things like that. I who all my life, have only been trying to do the best I could for you.

(pp. 219–20)

The contrast in wisdom and integrity of the two characters lies at the heart of the play.

In terms of character, dialogue and stage action the foregoing analysis is pressed as far as may be towards an interpretation of Ibsen's pattern of the sin of Cain and its consequences. There remains, however, one further possible line of enquiry; the nature imagery from the realm of myth which Ibsen uses at the end of certain plays concerning guilt. Without, it must be repeated, implying that Ibsen was drawing on a knowledge of anthropology or systematic psychology which cannot possibly have been his, it would be perverse not to give consideration to the mythopoeic material which does, in fact, cohere in his most powerful plays. He was a great poet and used the archetypal material which has been the poet's stock in trade through the ages. In *Brand*, *Rosmersholm* and *When We Dead Awaken* he seems to be presenting death in ecstasy, a death which might be interpreted either as a prelude to resurrection or as an assertation of absolute values independent of time. This is not the case in *Peer Gynt* or in any of

the plays of Ibsen's 'middle period', and only doubtfully so in
the *Master-Builder* and *John Gabriel Borkman*. In the other
plays mentioned the sense of a peculiar significance is associated with death by water or on a mountain.

The strongest sense of ecstasy is felt in *Rosmersholm* where
the lovers die by drowning, and the relevance of this to
ceremonial initiation has already been suggested. Water is an
ambivalent symbol; the waves from which Aphrodite rises to
bring love and life are also the waters of death, crossed by the
mythic poet heroes from Gilgamesh to Orpheus and to Dante,
but fatal to lesser mortals. Tertullian stresses the importance
of water to the Christian:

> habes, homo, inprimis aetatem venerari aquarum,
> quod antiqua substantia; dehinc dignationem,
> quod divini spiritus sedes, gratior scilicet ceteris
> tunc elementis.
>
> (*De Baptismo*, 111)

Chrysostom interprets its ambivalence:

> In Baptism are fulfilled the pledges of our covenant with God;
> burial and death, resurrection and life; and these take place all at
> once. For when we emerse our heads in the water, the old man is
> buried as in a tomb below and wholly sunk for ever; then as we
> raise them again, the new man rises in its stead.[*]

In Paleolithic days, we are told, 'the spiral was a symbol of
water and lunar fertility'.[†] In the mythologies of India,
Polynesia and America this significance persists:

> Immersion in water symbolises a return to the preformal, a total
> regeneration, a new birth, for immersion means a dissolution of
> forms, a re-integration into the formlessness of pre-existence; and
> emerging from the water is a repetition of the act of creation in
> which form was first expressed.[‡]

[*] Oxford, 1848.
[†] *Patterns in Comparative Religion*, Mircea Eliade, Sheed & Ward,
1958, p. 189.   [‡] Ibid., p. 188.

From this it must follow that water can symbolise both death and rebirth. In our own day the symbol has been re-stated by Jung.

> From water comes life; . . . All that is living rises as does the sun, from the water, and at evening plunges into the water. Born from the springs, the rivers, the seas, at death man arrives at the waters of the Styx in order to enter upon 'the night journey on the sea'. The wish is that the black water of death might be the water of life; that death, with its cold embrace, might be the mother's womb; just as the sea devours the sun, but brings it forth again out of the maternal womb.*

The association of an all-powerful creator with height appears to be so ubiquitous that even to mention it may seem banal. Anthropologists are divided as to whether the sky itself was first thought of as divine and thereafter sanctified the beings who were believed to inhabit it, or whether the sanctity of heaven is owed to the fact that a supreme Being was originally conceived as dwelling in it. In either case both Aryan and Semitic religious thought has conditioned us to take for granted that we praise God 'in the height'. Professor Edwin Bevan† has surveyed this symbol of the godhead as it is found in linguistic metaphor and mythical story in Europe—both Christian and pre-Christian—in Asia, in Africa and in America. Since God dwells in the sky, to climb the mountain must be a way of reaching him, and mountains as well as water appear in mythic cosmogonies as ways of reaching another world or another way of life. Both are connected with those 'rites of passage' which in primitive societies effect or accompany man's entry on the various stages of his life's journey. The image of the mountain is closely associated with that of the stairs or ladder which in the days before 'the fall' linked the world of men to that of the gods, as it did in Jacob's dream. Mircea

* C. G. Jung, *Psychology of the Unconscious*, trans. Hinkle, Kegan Paul, 1915.

† *Symbolism and Belief*, Gifford Lectures 1933–4, Allen & Unwin, 1938; Fontana Press, 1963.

Eliade writes that 'to die' in Assyrian could also mean 'to clutch the mountain', and in relating this interpretation of the image to that made by Freud he continues:

Even the purely sexual signification that Freud discovered does not contradict the more comprehensive symbolism of the staircase. The sexual act itself constitutes a 'rite of passage'. To infer that the patient who is mounting a staircase in a dream is thereby gratifying a sexual desire . . . is still a way of saying that . . . the patient is struggling to get out of a situation in which he is 'stuck'—a sterile, negative situation. *

In an earlier book† Eliade, in discussing the symbol of a mountain, tree or column situated at the centre of the world, describes an ancient Indian ritual which is relevant to a study of Ibsen's imagery.

In Vedic India the sacrificial stake (yupa) is made of a tree . . . Communication between the Heaven and Earth becomes possible by means of this pillar. He who makes the sacrifice does indeed go up to heaven, alone or with his wife, . . . While setting up the ladder, he says to his wife: 'Come, let us go up to Heaven!' She answers: 'Let us go up!' (*Sat. Br.* V 2, 1, 9) and they begin to mount the ladder. At the top while touching the head of the post, the sacrificer cries out: 'We have reached Heaven!'

(*Taittiriya Samhita, Sat. Br.*)

This is a true parallel to the situations in which Solness, Borkman and Rubek attempt to escape the limitations of mortality. Solness succeeds in climbing his tower, but he falls from it to his death, and Borkman, although he escapes from his prison home, dies with the mountains still far ahead—perhaps out of reach because he insists on seeking them alone. The imaginative impact of the plays' last moments suggests

* M. Eliade, *Myths, Dreams and Mysteries*. Harvill Press, 1960, pp. 116–17. Originally published as *Myths, Rêves et Mystères*, Gallimand, 1957.

† *Images and Symbols*, Harvill press, 1961, p. 45. Originally published as *Images et Symboles*, Gallimand, 1952.

that for Rosmer and Rubek the end is different, and although
Ibsen never makes an explicit statement that the price of
blood will not be exacted in full from every Cain, yet the
possibility of this is immanent in the imagery of at least these
two plays though absent from their overt statement, and the
fact may be a partial explanation of their continued appeal to
man's dramatic imagination.

Note

In connection with the stories of two lovers another symbol is
of interest. In close association with myths concerning death
by water are those concerning death, or apparent death,
through being swallowed by a monster. The whale saved
Jonah from death by water. By entering—actually in an initiation ceremony—the body of a giant ancestor or an animal monster, the hero both dies and re-enters the womb to be born again.

In discussing the symbolism of initiating ceremonies,
Mircea Eliade* says:

> The darkness that reigns in the interior of the monster corresponds
> to the cosmic Night, to the Chaos before the creation. In other words
> we are dealing here with a double symbolism: that of death . . . and
> consequently of the end of time, and the symbolism of the return to
> the germinal mode of being which precedes all forms and every
> temporal existence. Upon the cosmological plane, this double sym-
> bolism refers to the *Urzeit* and the *Endzeit*.

It is tempting to compare the death in love of John and
Rebecca with those of Romeo and Juliet and Antony and Cleopatra. It will be apparent that Shakespeare, whose lovers die
in the enclosure of a 'monument', either the Capulet's or
Cleopatra's, is presenting the 'monster' form of the initiatory
death myth, whereas Ibsen confines himself to the form of
death by water alone. To the author it appears however that by
the dramatist of the nineteenth century as by him of the
sixteenth, the mystery by which death is conquered in ecstasy
is once again presented to our eyes.

* Ibid., p. 223.

CHAPTER 4

AUGUST STRINDBERG:
The Appearance of Eastern Mythology

> Spin him round and send him flying
> Down to hell a Manichee.
>
> R. BROWNING, *Soliloquy in a Spanish Cloister*

THE strife of opposites is an obsessive *motif* in Strindberg's work. He uses both Cain and Esau as types of the rejected man and identifies both with himself, but in spite of this use of Old Testament typology the version of the myth of the warring brothers which is most in tune with his own imagination is not that of Genesis but rather that of the Zoroastrian heresy of Zurvanism.

In the system of Zurvanism . . . Endless Time is expressly put forward as the ultimate and supreme principle, as the primal source from which arose all things, including the two warring powers of good and evil. Endless Time splits in two thus creating the powers of Good and Evil, his twin sons,—who belong to each other but must forever combat each other. . . . Here cosmic historical time . . . is the basic power of history itself, endowed with divine and demonic, creative and destructive forces.*

This image of the primordial figures of victim and executioner as the conflicting parts of one precedent unity is central in Strindberg's work, for although Strindberg habitually projects the evil which he fights onto the figure of a woman, this does not make both his male and female dramatic antagonists less

---

* Ernst Cassirer, *The Philosophy of Symbolic Forms*, Vol. II, *Mythical Thought*, Yale University Press, 1955, pp. 117–18.

parts of himself. His many couples are so many projections of his own divided mind.

This essentially dualistic philosophy is presented under a number of different images. Occasionally it is figured as the contrast between light and darkness:

'Have you noticed,' asks the Stranger, 'that before the sun rises, a feeling of awe takes hold of mankind? Are we children of darkness, that we tremble before the light?' (*Road to Damascus*, p. 93)

More often, however, Strindberg contemplates the material universe with nausea rather than with awe. All his creative work is marked by an extreme dynamic energy, together with a no less extreme sensory acuteness. This last appears to conduce to a loathing of grease, slime and stench equalled only, perhaps, by Shakespeare's disgust at slavering dogs. In dirt and in the *trivia* of everyday living Strindberg finds the means to objectify his shrinking horror of his own flesh and his anguish at man's inability ever to apprehend the truth which his own nature yet compels him to seek.

DAUGHTER: (*of Indra*) Go back? To the stove and the cabbage and the baby clothes?

LAWYER: Yes. And it's washing-day—the big wash when all the handkerchiefs have to be done.

DAUGHTER: I would rather die. . . . It is not easy to be human.
(*A Dream Play*, p. 238.)*

The fresh air which might bring life and joy into the home is either polluted or excluded; the demands of the body destroy the spirit.

(*Kristin, the maid, is pasting strips of paper along the edge of the inner window.*)

KRISTIN: I paste, I paste.

* Except *The Road to Damascus*, all plays referred to are to be found in *Six Plays of Strindberg*, trans. E. Sprigge, Mayflower Publishing Co, N.Y.

DAUGHTER: You are shutting out the air. I am suffocating.

KRISTIN: Now there's only one small crack left.

DAUGHTER: Air, air! I cannot breathe.

KRISTIN: I paste, I paste.

LAWYER: That's right Kristin. Warmth is precious.

(*Kristin pastes the last crack.*)

DAUGHTER: Wretched, wretched beings . . .

KRISTIN: I paste, I paste!

(*The Lawyer standing in the doorway, nervously fingers the handle.*)

DAUGHTER: Oh, how that handle squeaks! It is as if you were twisting my heart-strings.

LAWYER: I twist, I twist!

(pp. 218–22)

Although in the original form of Zoroastrianism the brothers were both creative forces, so that the universe presented an original dualism and existed from the beginning as Good and Evil, in the later Zurvanism the whole material universe was held to have been contaminated by the wicked twin and was therefore identified with Evil. The gnostic, Mani, developed this dualism further and firmly equated the Good with spirit and the Wicked with matter. In Mani's own words, as they are recorded, we read: 'Two beings were at the beginning of the world, the one Light, the other Darkness.'* Professor Hans Jonas, who quotes this, expands it as follows: 'The duality of darkness and light coincides with that of "this world" and "the other world", since darkness has embodied its whole essence and power in this world which now therefore is *the* world of darkness.' In the teaching of Mani and his successors man is held to be created by Darkness to be used in the fight against Light.

The human body is of devilish substance, and . . . also of devilish

* From 'The Fihrist'—quoted in *Gnostic Religion*, H. Jonas, Beacon Press, 1958, p. 57.

design. Here the Manichaean hostility to body and sex . . . is provided with a mythological foundation . . . The creation of Eve had a special purpose . . . 'to her they [the demons] imparted their concupiscence in order to seduce Adam'.

Since any action in the material universe involves commerce with evil, an extreme and ascetic quietism became the mark of the 'Elect' among the Manichees, and their attitude to the body, and to woman, is extraordinarily close to Strindberg's.

The fiercest form of the conflict between flesh and spirit appeared to Strindberg to be roused in man by his own sexuality, and the sexual relationship becomes for him, therefore, the central symbol of the dichotomy he perceived in human nature. In *The Father* he is concerned entirely with the dramatisation of the war between man and woman, and the man's defeat is symbolised by the figure of the Captain, immobilised and helpless in the strait-jacket to which his love for woman, as wife and as mother, has betrayed him.

LAURA: Adolf, look at me! Do you believe I'm your enemy?

CAPTAIN: Yes, I do. I believe all you women are my enemies. My mother did not want me to come into the world because my birth would give her pain. She was my enemy. She robbed my embryo of nourishment, so I was born incomplete. My sister was my enemy when she made me knuckle under to her. The first woman I took into my arms was my enemy. She gave me ten years of sickness in return for the love I gave her. When my daughter had to choose between you and me, she became my enemy. And you, you, my wife, have been my mortal enemy, for you have not let go your hold until there is no life left in me.

(pp. 54–5)

It is, however, the conflict of male and female impulses within the microcosm of the individual which Strindberg uses to mirror most subtly the conflict between the twin forces of Good and Evil which, in his eyes, condition the universe. Perhaps his greatest success in the creation of such a divided soul is the heroine of *Miss Julie*, and it is at first sight curious that such a misogynist should achieve this triumph of imaginative analysis and reconstruction in the portrait of a woman. It seems that the fraction of extra 'distance' from his subject gave him the control necessary for the completely successful objectivisation of his personal experience. *

JULIE: . . . For that matter everything is strange. Life, human beings, everything, just scum drifting about on the water until it sinks – down and down. That reminds me of a dream I sometimes have, in which I'm on top of a pillar and can't see any way of getting down. When I look down I'm dizzy; I have to get down, but I haven't the courage to jump. I can't stay there and I long to fall, but I don't fall. There's no respite. There can't be any peace at all for me until I'm down, right down on the ground. And if I did get to the ground I'd want to be under the ground . . . Have you ever felt like that?

(pp. 83–4)

It is the fulfilment of her dream, in her seduction by the valet, Jean, which destroys her.

JULIE: Do you think I'm going to stay under this roof as your mistress? With everyone pointing at me. Do you think I can face my father after this? No. Take me away from here, away from this shame, this humiliation. Oh my God, what have I done? My God, my God! (*Weeps.*)

JEAN: So that's the tune now, is it? What have you done? Same as many before you.

JULIE: (*hysterically*) And now you despise me. I'm falling, I'm falling.

(p. 93)

In her distress she prepares to elope with her lover, but he kills her greenfinch, and, as she sees the bird dead on the chopping block, she recognises in it not only her lost innocence but

* Contrast the rancour and melodrama which flaw in places the characterisation of the Stranger in *The Road to Damascus*.

also her lost soul. It is this deeper insight into her true condition which brings her to despair.*

JULIE: No, I won't go yet. I can't . . . I must look. . . . You don't think I can bear the sight of blood. You think I'm so weak. Oh, how I should like to see your blood and your brains on a chopping-block! I'd like to see the whole of your sex swimming like that in a sea of blood.

(p. 107)

Finally she obeys Jean's demand to kill herself:

JULIE: Thank you. I am going now—to rest. But just tell me that even the first can receive the gift of grace.

JEAN: The first? No, I can't tell you that. But wait . . . Miss Julie, I've got it! You aren't one of the first any longer. You're one of the last.

JULIE: That's true. I'm one of the very last. I *am* the last. . . . And the first shall be last . . .

(pp. 113–14)

Julie is destroyed by the sexuality of her own nature because it is impossible for her, as it was for her creator, to accept it.

In no other play does Strindberg show the conflict between love and loathing of the body by means of the character of a woman. In his other plays the divided personality is always male, and the women are either figures of incredible saintliness—the wish-fulfilments of an adolescent's dream—or else vampires, wholly identified with matter and therefore with evil. Even the Lady in *The Road to Damascus*,† who is allowed more insight into reality and a less selfish scale of values than most of Strindberg's women, would destroy the Stranger's only hope of redemption if he remained with her.

---

* The choice of the pet to be destroyed makes the act more than an example of wanton brutality. The spirit leaving a man's body in the form of a bird is one of the earliest emblems of death used by man.

† English Version by Graham Rawson, Jonathan Cape, 1939; re-issued 1958.

LADY: Do you want me to leave you?

STRANGER: If you do, I shall die.

LADY: And, if I stay, it's I who'll die.

STRANGER: Then let's die together and live out our life in a
higher life; . . . .

LADY: I'd like to die, and yet I don't want to . . .

STRANGER: . . . there are moments when . . . I feel your hatred
like suffocating smoke.

LADY: And I feel my heart creeping from my breast, when you are
angry with me.

STRANGER: Then we must hate one another.

LADY: And love one another too.

STRANGER: And hate because we love.

(pp. 254–5)

Whatever the form of the conflict, Strindberg is obsessed by
the guilt of man's failure to resolve it.

STRANGER: I am Cain, you see, and am under the ban of mysterious powers, who permit no mortals to interfere with their work
of vengeance. You see this mark on my brow? (*He removes his hat.*)
It means: 'Revenge is mine, saith the Lord.'

LADY: Does your hat press?

(p. 125)

The point is clear enough, although it can perhaps be dan-
gerous to produce a myth so literally in 'modern dress'!

The Road to Damascus is, among other things, a myth of
the double guilt following commission of the two primordial
sins, the sin of aggression and the sin of sensuality. The
Stranger – an early example of the 'anti-hero' – is haunted in
his search for redemption by memory of an early sin, which is
only brought to light at the end of the Trilogy. It proves to be
one of the most curious of all versions of the myth which, in
Genesis, uses the symbol of Abel's blood crying from the

I

ground. As a very young child, the Stranger had torn a page from his story-book and hidden the damaged volume behind a wardrobe which he imagined to be immovable. Months later, however, the book was discovered by the adults, and another child was falsely accused and punished. The incident, which reads like an actual memory, is completely truthful to a child's experience, but, touching and convincing as it is at a naturalistic level, it proves unable to bear with complete success the weight of symbolism laid upon it. The fear owing to which the wrongdoing was concealed and the horror at its apparently supernatural discovery, are present but never fully communicated.

Strindberg repeats the pattern of the false accusation with the roles reversed when the Stranger, in the person of his *alter ego* 'Caesar', suffers confinement as a madman because his friend does not reveal the truth. A second *alter ego*, the Beggar, suggests that the only way to escape both guilt and punishment, to be neither victim nor executioner, is to contract out of all meaningful activity.

BEGGAR: I have always succeeded in everything I've undertaken, because I've never attempted anything . . . Life has given me all I asked of it but I never asked anything.

(p. 32)

Once the Beggar had been concerned in the original fratricidal strife; indeed his identification with the Stranger is betrayed by their common mark. The Stranger has already told the Lady:

You see this scar on my forehead? That comes from a blow my brother gave me with an axe, after I'd struck him with a stove.

(p. 29)

When he meets the Beggar he asks:

What's that scar on your forehead?

BEGGAR: I got it from a near relation.

STRANGER: Now you frighten me! Are you real?

(p. 32)

This unsavoury *doppelgänger* voices, during the first two parts of the Trilogy, most of the wisdom which Strindberg amassed, but could not apply, during his own journey to Damascus, but in Part III he does not appear, and his place is taken by the Tempter with whom the Stranger has already identified himself by his truly Luciferian pride.

BEGGAR: Bow yourself or break!

STRANGER: I cannot bow!

BEGGAR: Then break.

(The Stranger falls to the ground.)

(p. 160)

His physical likeness to Satan had also been remarked on.[*] The Tempter, when he appears, expresses all the cynicism and despair which prevent the Stranger's redemption from the flesh. Together they seek, for a time, not redemption but justification, and attempt to place the responsibility for evil directly on the Creator, as was done in the Zurvanite myth.[†] The search for the original guilt is pursued in the trial of a young man for a *crime passionnel* in which the Tempter acts as advocate for the accused. He traces back true responsibility for the murder through a long sequence of guilty persons until he reaches Adam, and then continues:

> Who was Adam's seducer! . . . Eve! come forward, Eve, Eve! . . . Now, Mother Eve, it was you who seduced our father. You are the accused: what have you to say in your defence?
>
> EVE: *(simply and with dignity)* The serpent tempted me!
>
> TEMPTER: Well answered! . . . Let the serpent come forward . . .

---

[*] Strindberg must be presumed to have cultivated deliberately his own physical resemblance to the conventional Mephistopheles.

[†] v. supra, p. 123.

Here you can see the seducer of us all. Now, serpent, who was it that beguiled you?

ALL: (*terrified*) Silence! Blasphemer!

The only answer is a thunder-clap, and the Tempter concludes:

> If the serpent is to blame then we're comparatively innocent. . .
> The Court of Justice has dissolved like smoke.
>
> (p. 239)

Strindberg, however, never achieves the abrogation of guilt and punishment in forgiveness, and his last plays show him seeking it only in the peace of death. His primary concern remains to the end the primordial strife of the twin brothers as interpreted by Mani, and he repeats it obsessively in his ruthless and horrifying dramas of the destruction of man by woman, the being who, as the Stranger declares:

> Bound me to earth—like the round shot a slave drags on his foot so that he cannot escape.
>
> (p. 243)

Always he had hoped to be granted his

> most secret desire and last prayer. Reconciliation with mankind through a woman. (p. 243)

Always he was disappointed; always there is the return to the bondage of the flesh.

STRANGER: I've never been able to understand how a kiss, that's an unborn word, a soundless speech, a quiet language of the soul, can be exchanged, by means of a hallowed procedure, for a surgical operation, that always ends in tears and the chattering of teeth. I've never understood how that holy night, the first in which two souls embrace each other in love, can end in the shedding of blood, in quarrelling, hate, mutual contempt—and lint.

(*The Road to Damascus*, p. 266)

The Stranger even refuses the possibility of parental love between him and his own daughter.

MIDWIFE: Your wife's given you a daughter.

MOTHER-IN-LAW: Don't you want to see your child?

STRANGER: No . . . . I'm afraid I'd get to love her, and then you'd tear the heart from my body. . . . Don't let that innocent child come near me, for I'm a man already damned, already sentenced, and for me there's no . . . forgiveness . . .

MOTHER: Exules filii Evae; on earth you shall be a fugitive and a vagabond.

STRANGER: Because I have slain my brother.   (p. 164)

The principal images in which Strindberg embodies hope of a healed and unified world is that of flowers. Spring is occasionally used, as in *Easter*, where its return is dramatised not only by reference to natural changes, but also, and less happily, by such matters as spring-cleaning, the removal of double windows and the putting away of goloshes, and where the play ends with a rebirth of human kindness and love. Soon I'll be recreated, and from the dark waters of Chaos the Lotus flower will stretch up her head towards the sun (*Road to Damascus*, p. 177). But more characteristically such seasonal imagery suggests only an unceasing repetition in which suffering is bound to predominate. In two plays, however, Strindberg does make an apparently determined effort to show both that spiritual beauty exists and that it springs from roots planted in the soil of the loathed matter. The great chrysanthemum of *A Dream Play* bursts into bloom above the miseries which alone appear to make its flowering possible.

DAUGHTER: . . . Ah, now I know the whole of living's pain! . . . the human heart is split in two emotions, by wild horses torn – conflict, discord and uncertainty. . . . Farewell!

(*She goes into the Castle. Music is heard. The background is lighted up by the burning Castle, and now shows a wall of human faces,*

questioning, mourning, despairing. While the Castle is burning, the
flower-bud on the roof bursts into a giant chrysanthemum.)

(p. 261)

The Lotus blooms, but no solutions are offered to the nightmare sequences of individual agonies and frustrations with which the play has been concerned; peace is not achieved even fleetingly in the here and now.

At the end of *The Ghost Sonata* the hyacinth imagery is directly related to Buddhism and therefore to a Manichean refusal of the world.

STUDENT: Do you know the legend of the flower? . . . The bulb is the earth, resting on the water or buried in the soil. Then the stalk rises straight as the axis of the world, and at the top are the six-pointed star-flowers . . . . This is why the Buddha sits holding the earth bulb, his eyes brooding as he watches it grow.

(pp. 296–7)

In the corner of the hyacinth room in which the student and the girl are talking the 'death-screen' is always visible. Now it is called for:

GIRL: Bring the screen. Quick, I am dying.

STUDENT: The Liberator is coming. Welcome, pale and gentle one. Sleep, you lovely, innocent, doomed creature, suffering for no fault of your own. Sleep without dreaming, and when you wake again—may you be greeted by a sun that does not burn, in a home without dust, by friends without stain, by a love without flaw. You wise and gentle Buddha, sitting there waiting for a heaven to sprout from the earth, grant us patience in our ordeal and purity of will so that this hope may not be confounded. . . . .

(pp. 303–4)

Whatever hope Strindberg may sometimes express of a flowering after suffering in some other manner of life, he offers none in this. Waiting in the chapel where the Stranger of *The Road* to *Damascus*, is to be received into a monastery, he and the Tempter are talking:

TEMPTER: Was life so bitter?

STRANGER: Yes. My life was. . . .

(*A woman enters with a child to be baptised.*)

TEMPTER: Look! A little mortal, who's to be consecrated to suffering. . . .

(*A bridal couple cross the stage.*)

And there—what's loveliest and most bitter. Adam and Eve in Paradise that in a week will be a Hell and in a fortnight Paradise again.

STRANGER: . . . I, too, once sat in the sunlight on a verandah, in the spring—beneath the first tree to show new green . . . and a white veil lay like thin morning mist over a face . . . that was not that of a human being. Then came darkness.

TEMPTER: Whence?

STRANGER: From the light itself. I know no more.

(p. 285)

The search for an escape from an intolerable situation becomes for Strindberg a death-wish: only in death or an image of death can he hope to re-unite the divided self and find peace.

TEMPTER: Are you ready?

STRANGER: So ready, that I have no answers left for you. . . .

CONFESSOR: (*advancing with a large black bier-cloth*)
Lord! grant him eternal peace!

CHOIR: May he be illumined with perpetual light!

CONFESSOR: (*wrapping the stranger in the bier-cloth*)
May he rest in peace!

CHOIR: Amen!

(p. 286)

Strindberg can only conceive of the unification of man's

divided personality as following the elimination of one of its elements. He accepts the assertion that 'it is profitable for thee that one of thy members should perish and not that the whole body be cast into hell', * even if the cutting off of the member is at the cost of life itself.

* Matthew, v. 29.

CHAPTER 5

J-P. SARTRE: The Existentialist Murderer

It is one thing to be admired, and another to be the guiding
star which saves the anguished.

S. KIERKEGAARD, *Fear and Trembling*

SARTRE never uses the complete myth of the warring
brothers, but elements of it are traceable in his dramatisations
of violent death, and their variations from the Christian
archetype are of particular interest. *The Flies,** a version of
the Oresteia of Aeschylus, is based on the different though
equally primitive myth of the murder of the mother by the
son, but it is relevant here in so far as it sets out, with the
clearness of a dramatic paradigm, Sartre's conception of responsibility and guilt.

Orestes makes his entry into Argos as the uncommitted
man. He knows that if he should become involved in the
society which could be his by virtue of his birth, there is one
deed for him to do: free the city from its usurping and evil
rulers, which means killing his mother and her paramour.
Orestes faces this choice; his freedom, as he says, 'crashed down'
on him 'like a thunderbolt', and he acted. Because he acts in
freedom he repeats Cain's original defiance of God. He says to
Zeus:

I am no criminal, and you have no power to make me atone for
an act I don't regard as a crime.

(p. 88)

This freedom is his anguish:

I was like a man who's lost his shadow. And there was nothing

* Translated by Stuart Gilbert, Hamish Hamilton, 1946.

137

left in heaven, no Right or Wrong, nor anyone to give me orders; no longer can I feel remorse, and I can sleep no more.

(pp. 96–7)

To his sister he makes the claim:

I have done my deed and that deed was good. I shall bear it on my shoulders as a carrier at a ferry carries the traveller to the farther bank . . . the heavier it is to carry the better pleased I shall be, for that burden is my freedom.*

(p. 79)

Electra on the other hand refuses her freedom and denies her share in both the horror and the triumph of the redemption of her city. She refuses to believe with her brother that 'Justice is a matter between men', and submits, cringing, to the judgement of Zeus. She hears the voice of her mother's blood crying from the ground in the persons of the Flies:

Listen! The sound of their wings is like a roaring furnace. They are all around us, Orestes . . . We'll never escape them, they'll follow us everywhere. . . . They're the Furies, Orestes, the goddesses of remorse.

(pp. 79–80)

Electra feels remorse for the murder of her mother, but her true guilt is not murder but the *mauvaise foi* which causes her to accept the judgement of God and of society and to deny the righteousness of her own freely conceived and executed action. Since Orestes has realised that God, the creator of the material universe, has no power over man, who was created free, he knows that there can be no supernatural sanction behind the Flies, and he can therefore ignore the threat of his mother's vengeance as securely as the primitive man, described by Sir James Frazer,† could ignore the ghost of his murdered victim once the mark of Cain had been stamped upon him.

* Contrast Ibsen's use of this image, supra, pp. 94, 96 and 103.
† Cf. supra, p. 12.

Orestes carries only the burden of his personal responsibility
with him into the future, not the burden of guilt, which he
considers to be an illusion fostered for pragmatic purposes by a
corrupt society, and he passes on his way leaving a saved and
redeemed city behind him.

> Farewell, my people. Try to reshape your lives. All here is new,
> all must begin anew. And for me, too, a new life is beginning. A
> strange life . . . Listen now to this tale. One summer there was a
> plague of rats in Scyros. It was like a foul disease; they soiled and
> nibbled everything, and the people of the city were at their wits'
> end. But one day a flute-player came to the city. He took his stand
> in the market-place. Like this. He began playing on his flute, and all
> the rats came out and crowded round him. Then he started off,
> taking long strides—like this. And he called to the people of Scyros,
> 'Make way!' And all the rats raised their heads and hesitated—as
> the flies are doing. Look! Look at the flies! Then all of a sudden they
> followed in his train. And the flute-player, with his rats, vanished
> for ever. Thus.
>
> (*He strides out into the light. Shrieking, the FURIES fling them-
> selves after him.*)
>
> (pp. 102–3)

Thus the existentialist Cain passes guiltless to his exile, and
the figure of the aggressor is absorbed into that of the saviour.
Thus the modern play reflects the conclusion of its prototype,
in which the Erinyes become the Eumenides and are made an
integrated part of the Athenian *polis*, while it rejects the
Semitic-Christian version of the myth which shows Lucifer–
Cain and Christ–Abel as for ever distinct. The Aeschylean and
Existential reconciliation of opposites is incompatible with a
system of absolute moral values and as alien to Strindberg's
Manicheism as to Ibsen's humanistic moralism. It contri-
butes to Beckett's ambiguity when it is hinted at in *Waiting
for Godot*, but in most drama written within the European
tradition it is repudiated as definitely, though not as vehe-
mently as it is by Euripides, in that supreme early statement
of human dichotomy and its tragic end, *The Bacchae*.

In *Crime Passionnel** the existentialist ethic is applied in a contemporary setting. The hero, Hugo, is instructed to commit murder, by the political party which he has recently joined. Since he is not really fully involved with the party this deed is not genuinely his own, and he is in fact unable to accomplish it until he finds his proposed victim, a man he greatly admires, in the act of seducing his wife. He then shoots in a flurry of personal emotion and finds that the deed has no significance for him at all. He neither achieves freedom nor feels remorse–only regret at the loss of the man he has killed.

> HUGO: I wanted to hang a crime round my neck, like a stone. I was afraid it would be very heavy. What a fool I was. It is light, horribly light . . . I don't even feel it. Neither round my neck, nor on my shoulders, nor in my heart . . . I liked Hoederer . . . I liked watching him and listening to him. I liked his hands and his face and when I was with him all the storms inside me died down. It isn't my crime that's killing me, it's his death.
>
> (p. 101)

We are here approaching the brother-murder in love which is dealt with more fully by other dramatists; here the play ends with the assassin dragged back into the existentialist pattern of heroism by his refusal to receive his life at the price of denying the political justification of what he did. He will not accept the directive of an external authority–the Party–and claims full personal responsibility for his deed:

> HUGO: A man like Hoederer doesn't die by accident. He dies for his ideals, for his policy, he is responsible for his own death. If I recognise my crime before you all, . . . if I agree to pay the necessary price, then he will have had the death he deserved.
>
> (pp. 105–6)

This 'Cain' thus at last becomes a pale but genuine reflection of Orestes.

* In *Three Plays*, trans. K. Black, Hamish Hamilton, 1949.

It is in *Loser Wins** that Sartre dramatises most fully the problems of Cain, although the undoubted power of this play stems not so much from its concern with political morality and individual justice as from the intensity of the erotic human relationships which are portrayed. The struggle between two women for power over a man and the subtly perverse colouring of their love are central in the first four acts of the play, and the relationship between the father and son is the driving force of the last and finest act. Around this triple struggle Sartre has woven a cloudy web of references to guilt and judgement which give the play an air of a greater political significance than it in fact possesses. From its diffuse comments and melodramatic situations, there emerges, however, a powerful theatrical image of the psychology of murder and its consequences to the killer. In his hero Sartre reveals the factors which can turn a sensitive and decent human being into a torturer and a murderer. The study merits comparison with those of Ibsen's guilt-ridden 'executioners', and although it lacks the sombre power over the imagination of those 'eminent Victorians' who tear themselves and each other to pieces without appearing even to disarrange their bustles and cravats, yet nevertheless Sartre's Franz von Gerlach–unlike his Orestes –is an individual whose fate is not only significant but deeply moving.

So long as Franz could imagine that Germany was being gradually but totally destroyed, his personal guilt was absorbed in that of his country, and her punishment was his:

The ruins gave me my justification. I loved our looted houses and our mutilated children. I pretended that I was locking myself up so that I should not witness Germany's agony. It's a lie. I wanted my country to die.

(p. 141)

When he began to realise that this punishment was an illusion he became afraid:

You will destroy me . . . Already my madness is falling into ruins.

* Trans. S. and G. Leeson, Hamish Hamilton, 1960.

It was my refuge . . . What will become of me when I see the light of day?

(p. 113)

Loser has indeed won all, and Franz is therefore driven to face his individual act and to attempt to assess it. His sister, Leni, offers him the existentialist creed, already dramatised by Sartre in *The Flies*.

LENI: I have only one judge–myself–and I acquit myself. . . .
   You will be invulnerable if you dare to state: 'I have done what
   I wanted, and I wanted what I have done.'

(p. 64)

But Franz could not accept this morality; he desired the approval of an external judge. By the millionaire ship-builder, his father, he was given in boyhood the illusion of both power and importance. He grew up to find that he had neither, and in the search for them he committed himself, contrary to his deepest intuitions, to Hitler's regime, until the boy who had risked his life to save a Jewish refugee became the man who tortured Russian prisoners on the Eastern front.

Remembering the earlier incident, he says:

FRANZ: Four of them held me down while the others beat him to
   death. What could I do? . . . Not even raise my little finger. A
   curious experience, but I wouldn't recommend it for future
   leaders. You never get over it. You made me a prince, father. And
   do you know who made me a king?

FATHER: Hitler?

FRANZ: . . . . I hated him before and after. But that day he
   possessed me.

(p. 139)

Years later he relived his own deed of darkness:

FRANZ: It's dark. Horror has not yet been let loose. I'll grab them

quickly. . . . I'll display my power by the singularity of an un-
forgettable act; change *living* men into vermin. . . . They'll talk.
Power is an abyss, and I see its depths . . . I shall decide life or
death with a penknife . . .

FATHER: Did they talk?

FRANZ: What's that? No . . . they died without talking.

(p. 146)

Since Franz cannot forgive himself he demands judgement
from another:

FRANZ: Judge me! . . .

FATHER: Would the torturer accept the verdict of the informer?

FRANZ: There isn't a God, is there?

FATHER: I'm afraid there isn't. It's rather a nuisance at times.

FRANZ: Then, informer or not informer, you're my natural judge.

(p. 141)

We seem now to be back in the world of John Rosmer and
Rebecca West where we are left alone to judge ourselves,*
and Sartre dramatises a self-judgement as ruthless as that in
the earlier play. At first, however, Franz is offered pity:

FRANZ: I was clean when I left you. I was pure. I wanted to save
the Pole . . . For God's sake, what did you think?

FATHER: My poor boy!

FRANZ: What?

FATHER: You asked me what I thought, and I'm telling you.

(p. 143)

But this does not satisfy him; he demands acceptance.

FATHER: And do you accept yourself?

FRANZ: What about you? Do you accept me?

FATHER: No.

(pp. 141–2)

* v. supra, p. 102.

But the judge who will not accept the criminal will not accept himself either. As Franz seeks to elude responsibility for his deed he finds, to his amazement, that his own father accepts it.

FATHER: And you, little prince . . . I made you a monarch, and today that means good for nothing.

FRANZ: Was I destined . . .?

FATHER: Yes.

FRANZ: To impotence?

FATHER: Yes.

FRANZ: To crime?

FATHER: Yes.

FRANZ: By you?

FATHER: By my passions, which I implanted in you . . .

(pp. 146–7)

The guilt of the murder is thus laid squarely upon the creator of the murderer; the deed is judged by the god who had made the man imperfect, and the god condemns both himself and his flawed creation, whom he pities but cannot save.

FATHER: Both your life and your death are merely *nothing*. You are nothing, you do nothing, you have done nothing, and you can do nothing. . . . Forgive me.

FRANZ: Forgive you for what?

FATHER: For you. . . . . I alone am guilty—of everything.

FRANZ: Well, I accept . . . On one condition only: that it is both of us, and at once.

(pp. 146–7)

Here the conclusion reached by Strindberg's Tempter in *The Road to Damascus** is no longer drowned by a thunder-clap, but openly stated. If justice is sought for, man's creator is found to be guilty of man's sin.

* v. supra, p. 132.

The double suicide takes place in a racing motor car, a modern image of the ship which carries the dead across the frontiers of the known world.

There is the sound of a car engine which grows louder then fades away. The head lights sweep the French windows as the car goes past.
(p. 150)

Franz' act of murder by torture is a parallel with the mother-murder of Orestes. It is chosen as the deed that will most revolt modern consciousness and exacerbate modern nerves: it is as near an absolute wrong as we can imagine. Does the play present the act as Franz' sin, or is his real sin not the act but his failure to accept it as inevitable and to override it? This last was what Orestes did successfully, but Orestes was sure of his course. He fully believed that his was a socially necessary task and was therefore secure in the sense of his own righteousness as he carried it out. Franz was essentially 'un-committed'—neither for nor against Nazism. He adored his country and loathed her rulers, or rather the part of himself which he believed to be good loathed them while another part revelled in their violence and prevented him from continuing to oppose it. Because of this failure he came to admit the truth of the words of the mutilated refugee woman which he repeats to his father years after he had first heard them:

God won't judge you by your deeds but by what you haven't dared to do, by the crimes which should have been committed, and which you didn't commit. You are guilty.

(p. 121)

But the judgement of his 'sins' of both commission and omission, for which the search is dramatised in this play, proves to be a fallacy. Such 'justice' is merely destruction, a punishment of others, or of the self, which is desired as the result of fear or inertia – in other words of *la mauvaise foi*. Franz certainly chose death because he dared not face the demands of the world outside himself, and he took his father with him

K

because the love-hate relationship between them was too strong to be broken, and the union in death, so passionately desired by the older man, was a source of joy also to the younger. Both motives are unrelated to any satisfactory conception of justice. Moreover the world is so organised that even when justice is genuinely sought the reverse of what the human mind conceives of as just is likely to occur: Loser, in fact, wins. The attempt to punish the criminal frees or enriches rather than destroys him. The most nihilistic of the Jacobean dramatists, while denying any lasting strength or reward to goodness, showed evil self-defeated in the end. Here even that is denied, and the only hope held out appears to be the possibility of accepting the evil with the good. Leni, however, who holds this creed is not herself strong enough to put it into practice but at last condemns herself to life imprisonment because of the acts—she would not call them sins—of her family, just as her father, who has pursued his own way without sign of moral scruple, at last finds satisfaction only in death. None of them find freedom or deny guilt.

But although it is possible to argue that the von Gerlachs should have carried their deeds triumphantly into the future as Orestes did his, yet the play's *ambiance* condemns the horrors committed by father and son in the service of the Nazi regime and contradicts much of Leni's existential morality or amorality. Whence does such a moral judgement spring? The blood of the Pole and the blood of the prisoners calls from the ground as did the blood shed in the primordial myths, and it is not unheeded: the murderers destroy themselves in their turn. The play's ending is essentially comparable to those of the stories of Alice Arden, George Saunders and Tom Merry dramatised centuries before. Murder exacts again its price of exile and self-destruction; it still has the earliest primal curse upon it as Claudius knew and as Macbeth discovered too late. In a generation for whom 'God is dead', humanity 'must perforce prey on itself'. Because the primordial belief in the guilt of murder was not imposed from outside by society, or even by religion, but rose out of the workings of man's own nature, it is still with us in this age of cynicism and despair. And in the play's honesty there is a ray of light: here where there is no hope of divine love or pity, or of a future life, the father and son are allowed, as Ibsen's lovers sometimes are, to die with their love intact; they are not divided by their shared crimes as were many of the Elizabethan murderers. The world of Altona is an easier one for most of us to enter than the world of Sartre's Argos; perhaps the dramatist's own passionate hatred of fascism led him to make this later play more true to the basic needs and impulses of which man's nature is made up. In any case the play's last words are a plea not for either condemnation or exoneration but for pity. After his death Franz' voice, addressing the future, comes over the tape-recorder which he has left behind him.

The century might have been a good one had man not been watched from time immemorial by the cruel enemy who had sworn to destroy him, that hairless, evil, flesh-eating beast—man himself. . . . I surprised the beast. I struck. A man fell, and in his dying eyes I saw the beast still living—myself. One and one make one—what a misunderstanding! . . . Happy centuries, you who do not know our hatreds, how could you understand the atrocious power of our fatal loves? Love. Hatred. One and one—Acquit us!

(p. 151)

Thus a fissure appears in the play's intellectual structure, and the living characters whom the dramatist has created, communicate an older message than that of the new morality of existentialist freedom. As in Ionesco's *Amédée*, guilt still proliferates in a world in which it should have no place, and the challenge of the corpse which grows in the bedroom must still be met.

CHAPTER 6

THE ABSURD UNIVERSE

Down we come
                    quick, but far
to the splendours
                    to the skill years
And the signed and fined grandeurs.
O yes, technique – but much more:
the good is still balanced
                    in the man – stones
    but it's a nice thing
as near a thing as ever you saw.

D. JONES, *The Anathemata*

i. INTRODUCTION

THE image of the blood which cried from the ground and was heard, gradually lost its power over men's dramatic imagination as it came to be mediated against a world view which made any moral certainties suspect. In the 'Western', the 'Whodunnit' or the Romance, the criminal is still inevitably discovered by chance or by his fellow men, but even the least sophisticated readers have ceased to think of such works as reflecting the world in which they live, and dramatisations of the myth have changed accordingly. Ibsen carried the moral assumptions of an earlier age into his plays, and his sinners mete out their own punishment in accordance with the old values, but John Rosmer's conviction that as there was no one else to judge him the sinner must judge himself, could not hold men's assent indefinitely. Strindberg's position is different, for while this self-styled demoniac suffers an intensity of guilt rarely surpassed, he never condemns himself. In his plays the means by which sin is punished vary: they may appear to be mechanically inescapable or dependent on human volition. But superhuman powers may be involved in this process – sometimes as onlookers, sometimes as agents, occasionally as life-givers. In terms of human morality the sinner's fate may be just, or unjust, merciful or cruel; it may be understandable or mysterious, but whatever its form its victims still demand to understand it, expect to understand it and suffer intolerable frustration if they do not do so.

We must turn now to the dramatists who write without hope of such a demand being meaningful, and who therefore never make it. It is Kierkegaard who first uses the word 'absurd' in the context in which it has now become familiar. In *Fear and Trembling** he writes of God's demand for the sacrifice of Isaac: here the universal moral law, comprehensible by the reason, which forbids murder, clashes with another demand—irrational and religious—which is to obey God. On this situation Kierkegaard's comment is: 'He (Abraham) believed by virtue of the absurd, for all human reckoning had long ceased to function' (p. 467). Such a belief is the salvation of the true 'knight of faith': 'By virtue of the absurd [Abraham] gets Isaac again. Abraham is therefore . . . either a believer or a murderer' (p. 67). Thus Kierkegaard arrives at the point where the demands of truth and ethics, i.e. the demands of religion and morality, clash. It is the same situation which fascinates Sartre, and which he has dramatised more than once. Kierkegaard is quite certain that the claims of truth, which are absurdity, transcend those of morality however rational. It is such faith that is for the believer a springboard, and he is: 'able to make from the springboard the great leap whereby I pass into infinity' (p. 47). Here we are introduced to the concept of the non-rational compulsive act by which the existentialist hero asserts his freedom, and, as for Sartre, the freedom won by faith is only to be enjoyed in anguish for, 'the pain is his assurance that he is in the right way' (p. 90). Summarising the core of Kierkegaard's attitude Fr. Martin d'Arcy writes:

He touches on the most sensitive nerve of human nature, its radical contingency, its subsistent agony, the constant contrast

* *Fear and Trembling*, trans. W. Lowrie, Princeton, 1941, and Anchor Books, 1954, to which the above page numbers refer.

between himself as part of the world of reason and order . . . and another part of himself which has to play the rebel and defy the rules and in that very irrationalism touch with longing hands a living God. He made the rent or schism in himself the very definition of life to such a degree that he would call true life a crucifixion.*

It is obvious that such an intense awareness of man's divided self could give new significance to the tragedy of the two brothers and the struggle between them, but for Kierkegaard the world of irrationality and anguish, of 'scandal' and constraint, was not a world of despair. The individual who truly 'exists' stands in a mysterious but direct relationship to the absolute which is God and in spite of sin and dread and sickness can live in the spiritual mode of being.

For many of the men whose work can be seen bearing the fruit of which Kierkegaard had sown the seeds, such faith has become impossible. The world of the absurd described so authoritatively by Albert Camus in *Le Mythe de Sisyphe*† is empty of the godhead. He begins by a direct statement of the central humanist problem concerning an irrational universe:

Il n'y a qu'un problème philosophique vraiment sérieux: c'est le suicide. Juger que la vie vaut ou ne vaut pas la peine d'etre vécue, c'est répondre à la question fondamentale de la philosophie.

(p. 15)‡

He is thus writing frankly as the moralist, the sociologist rather than the speculative or 'pure' philosopher, but for the student of that moral and social institution, the theatre, his work is not

* *The Mind and Heart of Love*, Faber & Faber, 1945; Fontana Library, 1962, pp. 327–8.

† Gallimard, 1942, *Collection Idées*, 1962; trans. J. O'Brien, Hamish Hamilton, 1955.

‡ There is only one truly serious philosophical problem and that is suicide. Judging whether life is or is not worth living amounts to answering the fundamental question of philosophy (p. 11).

the less valuable for that. Here is his description of the world as he sees it:

Un monde qu'on peut expliquer même avec de mauvaises raisons est un monde familier. Mais au contraire, dans un univers soudain privé d'illusions et de lumières, l'homme se sent un étranger.
(p. 18)*

De qui et de quoi en effet puis-je dire: 'Je connais cela!'. . . . Etranger à moi-même et à ce monde, armé pour tout secours d'une pensée qui se nie elle-même dès qu'elle affirme, quelle est cette condition où je ne puis avoir la paix qu'en refusant de savoir et de vivre, où l'appétit de conquête se heurte à des murs qui défient ses assauts?
(pp. 34–6)†

On this new 'chemin de la liberté' man moves in a 'douloureuse indépendance' as 'une âme pour toujours delivrée de l'espoir', but, albeit quite irrationally, he continues to live and even to enjoy life, although:

Son mot-clé, c'est le 'Tout est permis' avec la nuance de tristesse qui convient. Bien entendu, comme Nietzsche, le plus célèbre des assassins de Dieu, il finit dans la folie. Mais c'est un risque à courir, et devant ces fins tragiques le mouvement essential de l'esprit absurde est de demander: 'Qu'est-ce que cela prouve?'‡
(p. 146)

It is sometimes claimed that Camus, by asserting the essential value of life in spite of the pessimism inherent in a con-

* A world that can be explained even with bad reasons is a familiar world. But, on the other hand, in a universe suddenly divested of illusions and lights, man feels an alien, a stranger (p. 13).

† Of whom and of what indeed can I say: 'I know that!'. . . . A stranger to myself and to the world, armed solely with a thought that negates itself as soon as it asserts, what is this condition in which I can have peace only by refusing to know or to live, in which the appetite for conquest bumps into walls which defy its assaults? (pp. 22–3).

‡ His key-word is 'Everything is permitted,' with the appropriate shade of melancholy. Of course, like Nietzsche, the most famous of God's Assassins, he ends in madness. But this is a risk worth running, and faced with such tragic ends, the essential impulse of the absurd mind is to ask: 'What does that prove?' (p. 89).

sistent 'philosophy of the Absurd', is approaching the Christian view-point, and that he is proclaiming that the universe is not either chaotic or valueless, although its value is imperceptible to man without 'the leap' of faith. This is of course Kierke-gaard's meaning when he declares: 'Christianity is the absurd, held fast in the passion of the infinite'.* It appears, however, that Camus is rather seeking a viable humanistic basis for the acceptance of life as 'a good'. He nowhere flirts with Christian imagery or dogma and never appeals to the idea of a divine purpose in order to justify his assertion that it is better to live than to die. Strindberg's pessimism, however, has been by-passed by this determined irrationality and the way opened for a fresh dramatic assertion of the will to live.

ii. SAMUEL BECKETT AND FRANZ KAFKA: THE AMBIGUOUS DIRECTIVE

In the work of the greatest contemporary dramatist of the Absurd, Samuel Beckett, the myth of the warring brothers is central. The swaying dialectic of their relationship may image either the conflicts of the divided individual personality—fisseparous and self-destructive—or the processes of mutual destruction and assuagement which condition men's attempts at living together. In both the plays and the novels, the two opposing attitudes towards the irrationality of the universe—the Christian and the atheistic—are so closely and cunningly interwoven that to disentangle them is a task of curious and fascinating difficulty. A similar ambiguity informs the work of Franz Kafka whose two most famous novels, *The Trial* and *The Castle*, were posthumously published in 1925 and 1926.† Their view-point, technique of innuendo and some of the visual imagery are so close in certain respects to

---

* *Concluding Unscientific Postscript*, ed. W. Lowrie, Princeton, 1941, p. 169.

† *The Trial*, first published in German, 1925; trans. E. and W. Muir, Gollancz, 1935, Penguin Books, 1953. *The Castle*, first published in German, 1926; trans. E. and W. Muir, Secker and Warburg, 1930. Both novels have subsequently been dramatised and acted.

those of Beckett that a comparison is of interest. Edwin Muir, in his introduction to his translation of *The Castle*, writes:

Perhaps the best way to approach *The Castle* is to regard it as a sort of modern *Pilgrim's Progress*, with the reservation, however, that the 'progress' of the pilgrim here will remain in question all the time, and will be itself the chief, the essential problem. . . . Thus while Bunyan's hero has a clear goal before his eyes, and a well-beaten if somewhat difficult road to it, the hero of [*The Castle*] has literally almost nothing. . . . If any one wanted to estimate how immensely more difficult it is for a religious genius to see his way in an age of scepticism than in an age of faith, a comparison of *The Pilgrim's Progress* with *The Castle* might give him a fair measure of it. Yet hardly a fair measure perhaps. For Bunyan's mind was primitive compared with the best minds of his age, and Kafka's is more subtly sceptical than the most sceptical of our own.

(p. 6)

Kafka's world has been variously interpreted: Thomas Mann, in his introduction to *The Castle*, claims:

It is the most patient, obstinate, desperate wrestling with the angel that ever happened; and the strongest, boldest, most novel thing is that it is done with *humour*, which leaves utterly un-challenged the fact of the divine Absolute. . . . with utter sincerity, faith and submissiveness wrestling to win inside the incompre-hensible kingdom of grace.

Yet Mark Spilka, who quotes this in his recent book,* makes the *riposte*:

the hero . . . is the son who fights his Father to receive his love . . . in defiance of the very conditions imposed by his Creator. For this reason, his approach is not coupled with 'utter sincerity, faith and submissiveness' as Thomas Mann suggests, but is instead a matter of stubbornly repressed faith and unadmitted love, expressed through the disguises of anger, insult, deceit, argument, impudence and brash courage.   (p. 245)

* *Dickens and Kafka*, Dobson, 1963.

This does indeed place Kafka among the midwives of the 'absurd' society, and it is a comment which could well introduce the pairs of friends, enemies, brothers or doppelgänger who people Beckett's world. We are here concerned with just such an examination of the activities of the artist in the age of faith and in the age of scepticism, and Muir's comments on the mind of Kafka can be applied verbatim to that of Beckett. It has been said* that the principal theme of *Waiting for Godot*† is man's salvation, and perhaps that of *Comment C'est*‡ is his final damnation in the infernal mud of Dante's fifth circle. Both Kafka and Beckett write of an existence transcending the here and now; both men attempt to see and present that 'still point of the turning world' which has been the concern of all religious thought. Muir's assertion that Kafka believed in its reality and its accessibility to man is to be doubted. It is more than doubtful that Beckett reaches any such positive conclusion: he approves 'the guffaw of the Abderite',§ that there is naught more real than nothing, yet this may be a statement of Christian mysticism, and both men so construct their work that it does not specifically contradict orthodox Christian teaching. Such teaching has never declared that the mysterious ways in which God moves are accessible to the intellect of man. Even in the stable world of Elizabethan orthodoxy, the apparently senseless suffering of children was shown as disturbing if not 'absurd'. Gogo and Didi may be viewed as perfect representatives of Christian quietism, escaping by inaction from the sins into which the activities of Pozzo and Lucky inevitably plunge that unhappy pair.

And wait without hope
For hope would be hope of the wrong thing; wait without love
For love would be love of the wrong thing; there is yet faith
But the faith and the love and the hope are all in the waiting.‖

---

* R. D. Smith, Stratford upon Avon Studies, IV, Arnold.
† S. Beckett, Faber & Faber, 1956.
‡ Gallimard, 1963; trans. by the author as *How It Is*, Calder, 1964.
§ *Murphey*, Grove Press, 1938, p. 246.
‖ T. S. Eliot, *Four Quartets*, 'East Coker', Faber & Faber, 1944, p. 19.

In the very similar world they each inhabit neither Kafka nor Beckett expect to find justice as the word is ordinarily understood. For example in *The Trial* K. found that:

The legal records of the case and above all the actual charge sheets were inaccessible to the accused.

(p. 129)

The following passage from one of his earlier *épreuves* certainly calls to mind the more familiar figures of the bowler-hatted friends in *Waiting for Godot*.

There were only a few people in the lobby . . . they were sitting singly along a row of wooden benches . . . As there was no hat-rack in the passage, they had placed their hats under the benches . . . When those who were sitting nearest to the door caught sight of K. and the Law-Court Attendant they rose in acknowledgement. They did not stand quite erect, their backs remained bowed, their knees bent, they stood like street beggars. K. waited for the Law-Court Attendant who kept slightly behind him, and said: 'How humbled they must be!' 'Yes,' said the Law-Court Attendant, 'these are the accused men, all of them are accused of guilt.' . . . K. . . . turned to the nearest, a tall, slender, almost gray-haired man. 'What are you waiting here for?' K. asked courteously. But this unexpected question confused the man, . . . 'I'm waiting—' the man started to say, but could get out no more . . . 'You seem to put yourself to a great deal of trouble,' said K. 'Yes,' said the man, 'for it is my case.'

(pp. 73-4)

This is followed later by the ambivalent image of the justice, which is both pursuer and pursued:

A large figure rising in the middle of the picture . . . (K.) could not identify . . . 'It is Justice,' said the painter at last. 'Now I can recognise it,' said K. 'There's the bandage over the eyes, and here are the scales. But aren't there wings on the figure's heels, and isn't it flying?' 'Yes,' said the painter, 'my instructions were to paint it like that,' . . . 'Not a very good combination, surely,' said K. smiling.

'Justice must stand quite still, or else the scales will waver and a just verdict will become impossible.' 'I had to follow my client's instructions,' said the painter. . . . and as K. watched the delicate crayon-strokes . . . the figure . . . no longer suggested the goddess of Justice, . . . but looked exactly like a goddess of the Hunt in full cry.

(pp. 162–3)

In the first paragraph of *The Castle* K. arrived in the village at the foot of the hill on which the castle stands and finding there was not 'even a glimmer of light to show that a castle was there' he 'stood for a long time gazing into the illusory emptiness above him'. When he succeeds in ringing up the castle:

The receiver gave out a buzz of a kind that K. had never before heard on a telephone. It was like the hum of countless children's voices—but yet not a hum, the echo rather of voices singing at an infinite distance—blended by sheer impossibility into one high but resonant sound which vibrated on the ear as if it were trying to penetrate beyond mere hearing.

(p. 33)

Yet close on the abortive conversation which follows and in which K., in answer to his question 'when can my master [i.e. himself] come to the Castle?' hears the simple answer 'Never', a note of hope is struck:

A man came cleaving his way with rapid steps through the group, bowed before K. and handed him a letter. . . . His face was clear and frank, his eyes larger than ordinary. His smile was unusually joyous; . . . 'Who are you?' asked K. 'My name is Barnabas,' said he, 'I am a messenger.'

(p. 35)

The parallel passage in *Waiting for Godot* runs thus:

VLADIMIR: Was I sleeping, while the other suffered? Am I sleeping now? Tomorrow, when I wake, or think I do, what shall I say of today? That with Estragon, my friend, at this place until the fall of night, I waited for Godot? . . . I can't go on. What have I said?

(*Enter the Boy right. He halts. Silence.*)

BOY: Please, mister . . .

VLADIMIR: You have a message from Mr. Godot?

BOY: Yes, sir.   (pp. 90–1)

In each case the message leads nowhere.

Kierkegaard's influence on Beckett's imagination is also clearly indicated in *Waiting for Godot*. In *The Concept of Dread* Kierkegaard writes: 'To be lost in spiritlessness is the most terrible thing of all; for precisely this is its misfortune, that it has a relation to spirit which proves not to be a relation.' * This would be true of Macbeth; it is also true of Pozzo and Lucky. Shortly after this passage occur the following words:

Man when he is characterised as spiritless has become a talking-machine, and there is nothing to prevent him from learning a philosophical rigmarole just as easily as a political recitative or a confession of faith repeated by rote.

(p. 85)

Lucky's ludicrous and tragic outpouring of the draff of what remains of his mind does not carry lunacy much further. On the next page the correct audience reaction to Pozzo and Lucky is surely suggested:

Even though in spiritlessness there is no dread because this is excluded just as spirit is, yet dread is there nevertheless, only it is waiting . . . hidden and masked. Even the onlooker shudders at the sight of it.

(p. 86)

A few pages later Kierkegaard adumbrates an opposite state

* *The Concept of Dread*, trans. Lowrie, Oxford, 1947, p. 84.

which can well be applied to the waiting tramps at the end of the play: 'Even all the despair and all the horror of evil expressed in one word is not so horrible as silence' (p. 117).

The pairs of figures who torture and destroy—unless they occasionally redeem—each other, occur throughout the novels until they are epitomised in the narrator and Pim and the narrator and Bom, in the interminable sequence of executioner-victims who travail through the mud in Beckett's last horrific masterpiece, *Comment C'est*. Of the two pairs of men who appear in *Waiting for Godot* one is explicitly equated with mythical brothers. Pozzo who appears in Act I as the aggressor is now as feeble as his quondam victim. They collapse and Pozzo is lying blind and silent on the ground.

ESTRAGON: Are you sure his name is Pozzo? . . . We might try him with other names.

VLADIMIR: I tell you his name is Pozzo.

ESTRAGON: We'll soon see. (*He reflects.*) Abel! Abel!

POZZO: Help!

ESTRAGON: Got it in one!

VLADIMIR: I begin to weary of this motif.

ESTRAGON: Perhaps the other is called Cain. (*He calls.*) Cain!

POZZO: Help!

ESTRAGON: He's all mankind.

(pp. 83–4)

Executioner and victim have become one, as they were some-times held to be before the primal unity was self-divided.*

If Martin Esslin is correct in assuming that the letters M. and W. which begin the names of so many of the pairs in the novels represent Beckett's own initial in Greek—sigma—upside down or on its side, we may assume that both members of the pairs are emanations of the author's own person, used and abandoned in turn.

* v., pp. 193 and 240.

All these Murphys, Molloys and Malones do not fool me . . . I thought I was right in enlisting these sufferers of my pains. I was wrong. They never suffered my pains, their pains are nothing compared to mine, a mere tittle of mine, the tittle I thought I could put from me, in order to witness it. Let them be gone now, them and all the others, those I have used, and those I have not used, give me back the pains I lent them and vanish. *

Every man is both executioner and victim and to this Beckett returns in the superb prose poem *Comment C'Est*, but the relationship is complex. In *Waiting for Godot* the two tramps are not in conflict; on the contrary they bring each other such measure of consolation as is available in the human dilemma. The consolation may be due to an active giving of succour to another or to receiving it, and the passive recipient gives to his benefactor in turn, even if nothing else, the invaluable gift of companionship in suffering.

VLADIMIR: He'll tell me about the blows he received and I'll give him a carrot . . . I can't go on.

(p. 91)

Nevertheless, while they are together they can and do go on.

VLADIMIR: Pull on your trousers.

ESTRAGON: You want me to pull off my trousers?

VLADIMIR: Pull ON your trousers.

(p. 94)

What would happen if such a pair did indeed separate for ever is still left obscure until Beckett's latest play, *Play*.

Behind the actual couples in the play there looms the shadowy image of yet another—that of the two crucified thieves. This Beckett uses as did S. Augustine, who taught that men must never despair, for one of the thieves was saved, but likewise they must never exult for one of the two was damned.

* *The Unnameable*, Evergreen Books, Grove Press Inc., p. 305.

There appeared to be no rational explanation of this doubtful consolation, and to Beckett it was the more satisfactory as a symbol of the absurdity of the world because even the fifty-fifty chance of salvation was as much a matter for doubt, as the relative values of aggression and passivity, of giving or receiving.

VLADIMIR: But the other Apostle says that one was saved.

ESTRAGON: Well? They don't agree, and that's all there is to it.

VLADIMIR: But all four were there. And only one speaks of a thief being saved. Why believe him rather than the others?

ESTRAGON: Who believes him?

VLADIMIR: Everybody. It's the only version they know.

ESTRAGON: People are bloody ignorant apes.

(pp. 12–13)

In the novel *Molloy* the hero sees two men on a road. He identifies them with the thieves and they are instrumental in starting him on the quest for his mother, which is presumably a quest for the salvation which possibly one of the thieves attained. Molloy appears to have succeeded in reaching his goal, but whether this circular movement of return to his original home brought redemption or death or both together he had not discovered himself by the close of the book. 'In my end is my beginning.' It may well be so but the nature of both end and beginning appears to be inaccessible to the human mind.

End Game * is set within one man's skull. In the form of the two principal dramatic characters, this man wakes in the morning as the play begins and opens his eyes on the world without.

> Bare interior.
> Grey light.
> Left and right back, high up, two small windows, curtains drawn . . .

* Faber & Faber, 1958.

Centre, in an armchair on castors, covered with an
old sheet, Hamm.
Motionless by the door, his eyes fixed on Hamm, Clov.

(p. 11)

Clov gets his step-ladder, opens the curtains of each window
in turn and looks out; he removes the sheet which covers the
dustbins of Hamm's memories; he uncovers Hamm himself
and then awaits further orders. Hamm slowly raises himself.

HAMM: Me–(*he yawns*)–to play.

(p. 12)

These two characters present, in the fashion developed by
Descartes, Berkeley and Locke, the age-old imagined dichotomy of mind and body. The senses go into action and report
their findings to the mind, which is completely dependent
upon them for all knowledge of external reality. It seems to be
intended that Clov should be considered as, in some sense, the
son of Hamm, and if this is correct, the play is an idealist
statement asserting that the primary creation was of mind, not
matter. 'I think, therefore I am.' The body is condemned to
continual albeit futile and declining activity; Clov is unable to
sit down, and so cannot live other than the active life–a strange
avatar of the New Testament's Martha or Dante's Mathilda.
Hamm, on the other hand, lives in his imagination and
memory; he is blind and immobile unless assisted by Clov or
his mechanised extensions, the telescope and the gaff. He
cannot check the information he receives from Clov, though he
is completely dependent on him, both for his food and his pain-
killer. He would like to establish a love-relationship with Clov,
but this is, by the nature of the case, impossible.

HAMM: Before you go . . . say something. . . . A few words to
ponder in my heart.
CLOV: Your heart!

(p. 50)

L

Yet the couple are indissolubly connected, dependent on each other for their very existence.

HAMM: Gone from me you'd be dead.
CLOV: And *vice versa*.

(p. 45)

The obligation and the murder will equally be mutual, and neither will be left to mourn or to pay the penalty.

CLOV: This is what we call making an exit.
HAMM: I'm obliged to you, Clov, for your services.
CLOV: Ah pardon, it's I'm obliged to you.
HAMM: It's we're obliged to each other.

(p. 51)

At the end of the play Clov does attempt to leave, that is to say, to kill Hamm, but he cannot in fact go until Hamm releases him.

> (*Enter Clov, dressed for the road. Panama hat, tweed coat, raincoat over his arm, umbrella, bag. He halts by the door and stands there impassive and motionless, his eyes fixed on Hamm, till the end.*)

(pp. 51–2)

Hamm, however, concludes his part in exactly the way that Beckett's early master, Kierkegaard, says the intellectual tragic hero should: he is allowed 'to have and to keep the last word', and he refuses to expedite Clov's departure by an instant.

> HAMM: Cover me with the sheet. . . . No? Good. . . . Me to play. . . . Old endgame lost of old, play and lose and have done with losing. . . . Well, there we are, there I am, that's enough. (*He whistles. Pause. Louder. Pause.*) Good. . . . Father! . . . Father! . . . Good. . . . We're coming. . . . And to end up with? . . . Discard. . . . (*He sniffs.*) Clov! . . . No? Good. (*He takes out the handkerchief.*) Since that's the way we're playing it . . . (*he unfolds*

handkerchief) . . . let's play it that way . . . (*he unfolds*) . . . and
speak no more about it . . . (*he finishes unfolding*) . . . speak no
more. (*He holds the handkerchief spread out before him.*) Old
stancher! . . . You . . . remain.

(. . . *He covers his face with handkerchief, lowers his arms to
armrests, remains motionless.*)   (pp. 51–3)

Beckett's most horrific presentation of the myth of the two
brothers, the friend-enemies, the killer and the victim, is in
his last novel, *Comment C'Est.* Here are combined the intensity of the conflict within the Self together with the poignancy
of the imperfect contact with the Other. The peculiar desolation in which the two beings make fleeting contact might be
Beckett's implicit and sardonic rejoinder to the hope offered by
Martin Buber that 'relation', however hard of achievement, is
'a way leads up to God'. The parallels between the development of the child in Buber's classic, *I and Thou** and the
meeting of Beckett's original couple, can hardly be fortuitous.

Like primitive man the child lives between sleep and sleep . . . in
the flash and counter-flash of meeting. . . . Before anything isolated
can be perceived, timid glances move out into indistinct space,
towards something indefinite; . . . hands sketch delicately and
dimly in the empty air, apparently aimlessly seeking and reaching
out to meet something indefinite. . . . Little, disjointed, meaningless sounds still go out persistently into the void. But one day,
unforeseen, they will have become conversation. . . . the effort to
establish relation comes first–the hand of the child arched out so
that what is over against him may nestle under it.
                                                                   (pp. 26–7)

Comment C'Est presents the same primordial experience seen
through different eyes. After an unreckonable period of time
during which the unnamed narrator, having fallen from the
world of light above, drags himself through an equally unreckonable sea of mud, depending for survival on a jute coal-

* *I and Thou*, trans. Gregor Smith, T. & T. Clark, 1959 (2nd, revised
edition), p. 26; published in German 1923.

sack filled with tins of fish and one tin-opener, Pim and he at last meet. Their circumstances are strongly reminiscent of those of the souls of the Wrathful that Dante meets in the fifth circle of Hell.

> A marsh there is called Styx, which the sad stream
> Forms when it finds the end of its descent
> Under the gray, malignant rock-foot grim;
>
> And I, staring about with eyes intent,
> Saw mud-stained figures in the mire beneath . . .*
> (Inferno, VII. 106–10)

For a time there comes solace; the travellers touch each other, and at last Pim actually sings a strange little song, blowing bubbles through the mud to do so.

dans le noir la boue ma tête contre la sienne mon flanc collé au sien mon bras droit autour de ses épaules il ne crie plus nous restons ainsi un bon moment ce sont de bon moments . . . un petit air soudain il chante. . . .   (p. 68)†

passant sous la boue la main remonte. . . rencontre la bouche . . . tout ça remmue lèvres buccinateurs et poils c'est bien ce que je pensais c'est lui il chante toujours je suis fixé

Je ne distingue pas les paroles la boue les étouffe.   (p. 69)‡

But after this beginning all is changed, and the unnamed becomes the Cain, the torturer, the executioner. By blows and scratchings, woundings and pinchings, he proceeds to 'teach' Pim to behave as his tormentor desires:

---

* Dante, *The Divine Comedy*, 1: *Hell*, trans. D. L. Sayers, Penguin, 1949.

† In the dark the mud my head against his my side glued to his my right arm round his shoulders his cries have ceased we lie thus a good moment they are good moments . . . a little tune suddenly he sings (pp. 60–1).

‡ the hand approaches under the mud comes up at a venture the index encounters the mouth it's vague it's well judged the thumb the cheek somewhere something wrong there dimple malar the anatomy all astir, lips hairs buccinators it's as I thought he's singing that clinches it (p. 62).

première leçon thème qu'il chante je lui enfonce mes ongles dans l'aisselle main droite aisselle droite il crie je les retire grand coup de poing sur le crâne son visage s'enfonce dans la boue il se tait

(p. 77)*

At the end of the horrible process Pim's responses are thoroughly conditioned.

tableau des excitations de base un chante ongles dans l'aisselle deux parle fer de l'ouvre-boîte dans le cul trois stop coup de poing sur le crâne quatre plus fort manche de l'ouvre-boîte dans le rein

cinq moins fort index dans l'anus six bravo claque à cheval sur les fesses. (p. 85)†

The figures have assumed a life which inevitably recalls that of the damnation of the souls whom Dante saw

> Naked, with looks of savage discontent,
>
> At fisticuffs—not with fists alone, but with
> Their heads and heels and with their bodies too,
> And tearing each other piecemeal with their teeth.
>
> 'Son', the kind master said, 'here mayst thou view
> The souls of them that yielded them to wrath; . . .
>
> . . . others lie plunged deep in this vile broth
> Whose sighs—see there, wherever one may look—
> Come bubbling up to the top and make it froth.
>
> Bogged there they say: 'Sullen were we . . . .
>
> Sullen we lie here now in the black mud'.
> This hymn they gurgle in their throats, for whole
> Words they can no wise frame.
>
> (*Inferno*, VII. 111–126.)

* first lesson theme song I dig my nails into his armpit right hand right pit he cries I withdraw them thump with fist on skull his face sinks in the mud his cries cease end of first lesson (p. 69).

† Table of basic stimuli one sing nails in armpit two speak blade in arse three stop thumb on skull four louder pestle on kidney

five softer index in anus six bravo clap athwart arse . . . (p. 76).

Pim learns slowly, and the unnamed himself does not know why he follows this strange course. No adequate motive is needed for evil-doing, but with equal mystery and inevitability there follows its payment. The sequence is as automatic as it was in the imagined, ordered universe of the sixteenth century. At a given moment the couple separate. Pim crawls away, and the unnamed awaits the arrival of his successor who tortures him in his turn. And the unnamed realises that he and the beings he encounters are only single digits in an infinite series. In time he moves on once more:

à l'instant où je quitte Bem un autre quitte Pim . . . à l'instant où je rejoins Pim un autre rejoint Bem nous sommes réglés ainsi notre justice le veut ainsi. (p. 136)*

. . . bourreau toujours du même victime toujours du même et tantot seul voyageur abandonné tout seul sans nom tous ces mots trop forts presque tous un peu trop fort je le dis comme je l'entends. (p. 140)†

Gone is the element of luck, of the irrational, of the absurd, the fifty-fifty chance of salvation which had fascinated Beckett in the story of the thieves. We have returned to the rigidly ordered universe of the Middle Ages, though there is no sign that we have found once more its beneficent Creator. Hell is experienced indeed, but we are never led thence 'to look once more upon the stars' (*Inferno* XXXIV. 139).

'Pim, Beckett's generic other person, is the stable and ordering principle' of *Comment C'Est*, but as Professor Kenner continues:

a person cannot be silent, even voyaging through strange seas of thought; there is no inner silence. . . . Not even by retreating so far

* at the instant I leave Bem another leaves Pim . . . .
at the instant I reach Pim another reaches Bem we are regulated thus our justice wills it (p. 121).

† . . . tormentor always of the same and victim always of the same and now alone journeying abandoned all alone nameless all these words too strong almost all a little too strong I say it as I hear it (p. 124).

as may be within himself can he escape confrontation with the Other, since his very words shape alternate persons, his very musings subdivide himself. Not even by resigning himself, with Molloy, to 'senseless, speechless, issueless, misery' can he evade the symmetries and permutations that torment the mind.*

> Je suis la plaie et le couteau
> La victime et le bourreau.†

This isolation alone with a subjective 'other' is the last horror that a human being can be asked to endure. In *Happy Days*‡ we watch Winnie, immobilised in her sandpit, forced at last to face this loneliness because Willie, her 'generic other', may cease or have ceased to exist.

> Willie . . . May one still speak of time? . . . Say it is a long time now, Willie, since I saw you . . . since I heard you. . . . I used to think that I would learn to talk alone . . . By that I mean to myself, the wilderness . . . But no . . . No, no . . . Ergo you are there . . . Oh no doubt you are dead, like the others, no doubt you have died, or gone away and left me, like the others, it doesn't matter, you are there.
>
> (pp. 37–8)

At the end of the play although Willie can only crawl towards her and never reach her and can articulate only the first syllable of her name, she can still call her day a happy one for she is not yet alone. In *Play*§ the couple has become a trio which is destroyed by the tensions set up between its members.

Beckett's couples may be 'agglutinés pour les besoins du tourment', but better be Abel slaughtered by Cain, Lucky exploited by Pozzo, or even Pim tormented by the unnamed one, than survive in solitude to hear one's own voice dying away in inarticulate lament:

* *Samuel Beckett*, Hugh Kenner, Calder, 1962, pp. 189–90.
† Baudelaire, L'Héautontimorouménos', *Les Fleurs du Mal*, 1857; *Baudelaire*, Penguin Poets, 1961.
‡ Faber & Faber, 1962.
§ Faber & Faber, 1964.

. . . . C'EST MA VIE ICI hurlements bon

seul dans la boue oui le noir oui. . . . quelques mots oui quelques bribes oui que personne n'entend oui mais de moins en moins pas de réponse DE MOINS EN MOINS oui

bon bon fin de la troisième partie et dernière voilà comment c'était fin de la citation après Pim comment c'est.

(pp. 176-7)*

iii. JEAN GENET: THE REVERSAL OF VALUES

> At the moment of the 'consolarmentum' the imperfect
> member was made perfect to die.
>
> Written of the Cathari by Jean Guiton, *The Guiton Journals.*

Jean Genet—Sartre's 'Saint Genet'—carries the myth of the warring brothers to the highest imaginable pitch of intensity. He is obsessed, as Sartre has pointed out, by 'le couple eternel du Criminel et de la Sainte',† and he uses the Zurvanite prototype in which the antagonists are the warring parts of an original unity, for whatever the sex of his 'pairs', and however fantastic the disguises they assume, they consistently represent two elements of their creator's own schizoid personality. Moreover Genet puts his myth, as it were, into reverse: the sinner becomes the saint, Cain becomes Abel. The Gnostics in the re-action against orthodox Judaism were the first who had mythologised in this sense. They actually included a sect who called themselves Cainites, and some of their resentment against conventional morality has a curiously modern ring, as well as recalling the Romantic Satanism of the nineteenth century, represented, for example, in Byron's *Cain*.

This general Serpent is also the wise word of Eve. This is the mystery of Eden . . . This is also the mark that was set upon Cain,

---

* THAT'S MY LIFE screams good

Alone in the mud yes the dark yes. . . . a few words yes a few scraps yes that one hears no but less and less no answer

LESS AND LESS yes . . . good good end at last of part three and last that's how it was end of quotation after Pim how it is (p. 160).

† Sartre, *Saint Genet: Comedien et Martyr*, Gallimard, p. 564; trans. B. Frechtman, W. H. Allen, 1964.

whose sacrifice the god of this world did not accept whereas he accepted the bloody sacrifice of Abel; for the lord of this world delights in blood.*

In more fantastic terms the Hebrew God is himself divided into good and evil elements.

. . . Then Ialdabaoth saw the virgin who stood beside Adam. Senselessness filled him, and he wanted to let seed sprout from her. He seduced her and begot the first son, and similarly the second: Yahweh with a face like a bear, and Elohim, with a face like a cat. But one is righteous while the other is unrighteous. He set the righteous one over fire and wind; the unrighteous one he set over water and earth. These are the ones who up to the present day are called Cain and Abel among all generations of men†

In the Gnostic 'Harrowing of Hell' the Christian myth is again stood on its head:

When the Lord descended to Hades, Cain and those like him, the Sodomites, the Egyptians and those like them, and in general all the people who have walked in every compound of wickedness, were saved by him; they ran to him and were taken up into his kingdom. But Abel, Enoch, Noah, and the rest of the righteous . . . did not participate in salvation.‡

Murder, the sin of Cain, is claimed by Genet to be the most intense experience of living available to man, though he 'confesses' he never achieved it himself. It was not in his nature, he explains, but it remained with him for many years as more than a merely theoretical ideal. Sartre writes that Genet was never actually the lover of a murderer, but whether the poems dedicated 'à Maurice Pilorge, assassin de

* Hippolytus, *Refut*: V. 16. 9 f, quoted H. Jonas in *Gnostic Literature*, pp. 94–5.

† 'Secret Book of John', from *Gnosticism, an Anthology*, ed. R. M. Grant, Collins, 1961, p. 81.

‡ Marcian, ibid., p. 46.

vingt ans', express actuality or fantasy, their significance is the
same.

J'ai dédié ce poème a la mémoire de mon ami Maurice Pilorge
dont le corps et le visage radieux hantent mes nuits sans sommeil.
En esprit je revis avec lui les quarante derniers jours qu'il passa, les
chaînes aux pieds et parfois aux poignets, dans la cellule des con-
damnés a mort de la prison de Saint-Brieuc . . . Bref . . . je veux
ici, le plus doucement possible, tendrement, affirmer qu'il fut digne,
par la double et unique splendeur de son âme et de son corps, d'avoir
la bénéfice d'une telle mort. . . . Il fut éxécute le 17 mars 1939 à
Saint-Brieuc.*

Of the poems to the murderer which follow this dedication,
these verses may serve as example.

> Pour te plaire ô gamin d'une sourde beauté
> Je resterai vêtu jusqu'à ce que je meure
> Et ton âme quittant ton corps décapité
> Trouvera dans mon corps une blanche demeurs.
> O savoir que tu dors sous mon modeste toit!
> Tu parles par ma bouche et par mes yeux regardes
> Cette chambre est la tienne et mes vers sont de toi.
> Revis ce qu'il te plaît car je monte la garde.†
>
> (Marche Funèbre, VII.)

The murder which is accounted such a supreme experience is
not any casual killing: it may be a 'given' experience, suddenly
sweeping the actor away, like that of Yeux Verts, or it may be
an act for which the murderer has deliberately to induce a
state of trance like that of a witch-doctor, as is the case for
Solange. Murder committed as a means to a practical end, on
the other hand, can never have the value of the ritual act and
is unlikely to further even the immediate desires of the
murderer. When Lefranc tries to win Green Eyes by his
deliberate murder of Maurice, his act has no emotional impact

---

* Introduction to *Poèmes*, L'Arbalète, Paris.   † Ibid.

whatever on himself or on others. Society may exact the payment of a life for a life in both types of killing, but where
murder is regarded as a supreme assertion of a supra-rational
force there can be no question of a just punishment for it, and
indeed all social justice appears in these plays as a simulacrum,
like the disguised and padded judge of *The Balcony*.*

Murder to Genet is not only an assertion of vitality; it is also
a supreme assertion of love, for love cannot be content without
the complete assimilation of the loved one which only death
can ensure. Moreover, because the obverse of love is hate, the
murder of the beloved gives full satisfaction to the complete
love-hate emotion, the most intense which human beings can
experience. But such a relationship is continually thwarted by
the weakness induced in human beings by the tyranny of
society, as Solange admits: 'When slaves love one another, it's
not love.' Nevertheless when Genet wrote *The Blacks* he had
come to imagine a closeness in death of master and slave which
transcended in its intensity any other union accessible to man,
and this is achieved by the social outcasts who are personified
in the negro characters.

Genet's first play *Death Watch*† is set in such a prison as the
poems to Pilorge describe and embodies their scale of values.
Two murderers in the prison are awaiting execution. One is
the huge Negro, Snowball, who is to the whole community
what Green Eyes is to the three occupants of the little cell in
which the action of the play passes.

GREEN EYES: Here in the cell I'm the one that bears the brunt . . .
I need a strong back. Like Snowball. He bears the same weight.
But for the whole prison. Maybe there's some one else, a Number
One Big Shot, who bears it for the whole world.

(p. 32)

The other prisoners adore the men who have qualified by
murder and condemnation as their leaders.

* Faber & Faber, 1958.
† First published as *Haute Surveillance*, Gallimard, 1949; trans. B.
Frechtman, Faber & Faber, 1961.

LEFRANC: Snowball? He's out of this world . . . He shines. He beams. He's black but he lights up the whole two thousand cells.

(p. 9)

Their elevation to this role is part of a *mystique*; it has descended on them 'like a gift, like a grace', as love was said to do in happier days.

GREEN EYES: It's by its sweetness that you recognise catastrophe.

(p. 22)

You don't know the first thing about misfortune if you think you can choose it. I didn't want mine. It chose me. It fell on my shoulders and clung to me.   (p. 40)

It is in such an inverted hierarchy that Genet's first important play, *The Maids*, is set. Here he uses directly the fratricidal conflict in order to dramatise his theme. Sartre has pointed out the similarity of structure between the two plays:

Haute Surveillance . . . reprend très exactement le sujet des *Bonnes*, même hiérarchie: le mâle absent, dans un cas Monsieur, dans l'autre Boule de Neige; la divinité intermediaire, Madame ou Yeux Verts; et les deux adolescents, qui rêvent au meurtre, ne parviennent pas à le commettre, qui s'aiment et se haïssent et dont chacun est la mauvaise odeur de l'autre, Solange et Claire, Maurice et Lefranc. . . . Faux assassin Lefranc est un vrai traitre; Maurice au contraire trop jeune pour tuer, est de la race des tueurs; ainsi reforment-ils "le couple éternel du Criminel et de la Sainte"; . . . . or c'est justement ce couple éternel que Solange et Claire veulent former. *   (p. 564)

* *Saint Genet*; v. supra, p. 168. *Death Watch* . . . deals with exactly the same subject as *The Maids*. There is the same hierarchy: in one case, Monsieur, in the other, Snowball; the intermediate divinity, Madame and Green Eyes; and the two youngsters who dream of murder but fail to commit it, who love and hate each other and each of whom is the other's bad smell, Solange and Claire, Maurice and Lefranc. . . . Lefranc, who is a fake, is a real traitor; Maurice, however, who is too young to kill, is of the race of killers; thus they too form 'the eternal couple of the Criminal and the Saint'; . . . This is the same eternal couple that Solange and Claire want to form (p. 614).

The Maids,* which is the most perfectly constructed of Genet's plays, was the first to be performed, although it was the second to be written. It is a play about love—a love in which the desire to dominate is at war with the desire to submit, the desire to cherish with the desire to destroy, the desire to possess completely with the desire to give with equal completeness—that is to say a true love-hatred.

At the deepest level the warring elements exist in the one person. Solange longs to dominate, longs to perform the final act of aggression, murder. But such a capacity for triumph is not to be had for the wishing. Solange cannot alter the balance of forces within her own nature. The power to kill is a gift. After two failures Solange reveals her own psyche by awaiting in ecstasy her execution for a murder which she did not commit. Her sister, Claire, apparently so much more delicate and even fragile a creature, is in reality the stronger. Her attempted murder fails through chance only, and after its failure she is able calmly to drink the poisoned tea herself. She is 'le vrai dur', the 'Cain', the 'Mac', to whom the need to kill comes from within herself—she does not know how or why —and with the need, comes the faculty. As both elements of the love-hate situation may be found within the same personality, so the most highly charged object of the love-hatred may be this same self, loved because it alone registers the precious emotions, loathed because it is incapable of giving itself fully the satisfaction it craves. It is herself that Claire is abusing when in her role of Madame she abuses Solange:

CLAIRE: Avoid pawing me. You smell like an animal. You've brought those odours from some foul attic where the lackeys visit us at night.

(p. 10)

It is herself she loves as she looks at herself in Madame's mirror, wearing Madame's red velvet gown—her 'lovely

* Trans. B. Frechtman, Faber & Faber, 1957; paper covered edition, 1963 (to which page references in text refer).

Fascination'. Solange loves herself in her sister's beauty, and they both hate in each other their own 'bad smell'.

But *The Maids* is not a psychological analysis; it is an artifact, a piece of theatre, a brilliant play. It presents itself by means of visual and aural imagery, that is to say by characters, their visible actions and their spoken words. At the most obvious level of meaning the story shows us two maids cringing before a generous mistress with adoration, at the same time that they inform on her lover to the police and betray their jealousy of her power by taking it in turns to dress in her clothes and tyrannise over each other in her form. This is the level on which the play opens. Claire is standing in a petticoat by Madame's dressing-table, while Solange acts the part of Claire.

CLAIRE: Get my dress ready. Quick! . . . Claire! Claire! . . . Lay out my things. The white spangled dress. The fan. The emeralds.

SOLANGE: Very well Madame. All Madame's jewels?

CLAIRE: Put them out and I shall choose. (p. 7)

And the mimic bullying and cringing continues until the mistress's return interrupts it. At another level, however, the play is a more direct reflection of the Cain–Abel prototype, for the maids are sisters and in their disguise as mistress and maid (for the sister playing the maid is always the *other* maid, not herself) are equally concerned in their personal love-hate relationship, dominating and serving, cherishing and destroying, to the point where Solange—had she in fact been Solange-Cain, not Solange-Abel in disguise—would have repeated the primordial murder on her sister.

SOLANGE: Stop. I've got there . . . Down on your knees! Ah! Ah! You were so beautiful, the way you wrung your precious arms! Your tears, your petals oozed down your lovely face. . . . Don't yell! It's useless. Death is present, and is stalking you. Don't yell! I, who kept you the way they keep kittens for drowning. I, yes, I, who trimmed my belly with pins to stab all the foetuses I threw into the gutter! In order to keep you, to have *you* alive!

CLAIRE: Solange, Solange, come to yourself!

SOLANGE: To *your*self!

CLAIRE: Help!

SOLANGE: Stop yelling! No-one can hear you! We're both beyond
    the pale!

(pp. 35–7)

There is still a further level of interpretation to be considered, for Genet makes his image macrocosmic as well as
microcosmic. The attempted murder and actual suicide are
played out as rituals: the re-enactment of events *in illo tempore*,
where the truth of his being was not hidden from man but
was revealed in the actions of his ancestors when they were
still as gods. In other words, a mythical death is presented as a
Mass for the purging of all men's souls. The ways in which
this effect is achieved resemble the conventions of the Elizabethan ritualisation of revenge. Victim and executioner dress
for their parts and approach their climax by an established
ceremonial which has something of the nature of a dance or of
a play within a play. For the murder Claire wears her mistress's red velvet dress, chosen for her by her executioner.

SOLANGE: The red dress. Madame will wear the red dress.

CLAIRE: I said the white dress, the one with spangles.

SOLANGE: I'm sorry. Madame will wear the scarlet velvet dress
    this evening . . . The fall of your dress. I'm arranging your fall
    from grace.

(pp. 8–10)

And the dress is meticulously arranged. For the final suicide,
however, Claire chooses her dress, and it is the white one. She
puts it on over her maid's dress so that the black sleeves show.
Solange, who is the true victim and also the single mourner,
wears at the end her own short black dress, having removed
the white apron she wore over it when playing Claire earlier
in the scene. In the red dress Claire plays the role of the sinner,

fallen from grace and righteously slain. In the white she is playing a voluntary Iphigenia, dying, a virgin, for the sins of others. That they are her own also and that the slayer and the slain are, in each case, equally innocent and guilty is a necessary part of the pattern.

Claire knows the purpose of the masquerade to be death— mimed or real.

CLAIRE: You're taking revenge, aren't you? You feel the time coming when, no longer a maid. . . . (*increasingly carried away*) the time coming, when no longer a maid, you become vengeance itself.

(p. 11)

All the self-hatred which is the result of their frustration pours out like lava.

CLAIRE: (*as the mistress*) Start the insults. I said the insults! Let them come, let them unfurl, let them drown me, for as you know, I loathe servants . . . they're not of the human race. Servants ooze. They're a foul effluvium, drifting through our rooms and hallways, seeping into us, entering our mouths, corrupting us. I vomit you.

SOLANGE: Go on . . . Go on! I'm getting there, I'm getting there!

CLAIRE: . . . . your frightened guilty faces, your puckered elbows, your outmoded clothes, your wasted bodies, only fit for your cast-offs. You're our distorting mirrors, our loathsome vent, our shame, our drags! . . . Please! I can't go on . . . I've run out of insults. Claire, you exhaust me.

SOLANGE: Stop. I've got there. It's my turn . . . Down on your knees . . . Down! Down! . . . Crawl! Crawl! I say, like a worm . . .

CLAIRE: Solange, please, I'm sinking . . . We're out of our depth.

(pp. 34–6)

Part of the ritual is torture and Solange does in fact strike Claire with a whip. Sartre interprets the token thus:

De nouveau le faux est vrai et le vrai ne peut s'exprimer que par le moyen du faux. Et lorsque Claire appelle Solange 'Traînée', lorsque Solange, extasiée, s'écrie, 'Madame s'emporte,' *qui donc* insulte *qui*? Et *qui donc* ressent l'insulte avec cette volupté masochiste? . . . Et *qui* gifle *qui*? Cette gifle est un rite sacré qui figure le viol de Genet par le Male.*

Finally Claire drinks in actuality and willingly the tea she had poisoned for her mistress.

CLAIRE: Nothing exists but the altar where one of the two maids is about to immolate herself. (p. 46)

In the release which follows Claire's death Solange pronounces her epitaph while she awaits her own arrest for the murder she was unable to commit.

All the maids were present at her side—not they themselves, but rather the hellish agony of their names. And all that remains of them to float about Madame's airy corpse is the delicate perfume of the holy maidens which they were in secret. We are beautiful, joyous, drunk and free. (p. 43)

La réalité n'est qu' apparence, mais l'apparence révèle la surréalité.†
CLAIRE: We shall be that eternal couple . . . the eternal couple of the criminal and the saint. (p. 22)

The sense of universal reality corresponding to the unreality of the particular instance, is achieved by the fantastic hall of mirrors which Genet has constructed in his play. It is known that before it was first produced he demanded that the

---

* Once again the false is the true and the true can be expressed only by means of the false. And when Claire calls Solange 'You slut,' when Solange, *in ecstasy* cries, 'Madame is being carried away!' *who* is insulting *whom*? And who feels the insult with that masochistic pleasure? . . . And *who* slaps *whom*? This slap is a sacred rite which represents the rape of Genet by the Male. Sartre, op. cit., pp. 571 of French edition, pp. 622–3 of Translation.

† Sartre, op. cit., p. 307.

M

parts of all three women should be played by men, and that a
notice saying that this was so should be permanently fixed to
the side of the proscenium arch. He gave way on this point to
Louis Jouvet's objections, but the continual reminder that the
figures on the stage were never in fact what they purported
to be would have been a valid image of the play's essential
form. Even without this first term, however, the sequence is
sufficiently impressive. The actress is acting a woman who
is acting a maid who is acting a mistress. And the maid who is
acting a mistress is also a strong woman acting a weak woman,
and a woman full of hatred acting a woman full of love, who is
at the same time a woman full of love who thinks she is a
woman full of hatred. The actor or actress playing Solange is
at the end of the play impersonating a maid who is impersonating an executioner who is impersonating his own destined
victim. And so the fantastic chains go on, and always the last
observable reality is the reality within the divided mind of the
dramatist. Genet has admitted he has never committed the
'sin' he so passionately admired. He is Solange not Claire, and
it is for Solange not for Claire that our sympathy is finally demanded. Genet is compelled to believe that 'la toute-fille a plus
de vrai courage que le dur',* because he knows he is himself
'la toute-fille'.

Sartre quotes an epigram Genet made on himself and expands it thus:

'Jean Genet le plus faible de tous et le plus fort' . . . Genet . . .
se réfère a deux systèmes de valeurs opposés . . . Dans le premier
le Mal est le destin, le Mal pur . . . Genet n'est rien qu'un voyou,
crapuleux, tout juste bon à servir en esclave un maître rigoureux.
Dans le second Jean Genet, conscience froide et lucide, enchaîne le
criminel par ses paroles, par ses charmes, le mène a sa perte par
des trahisons parfumées. Mais chaque système implique l'autre . . .
Il faut qu'il (le criminel) conserve toute sa supériorité sur la Sainte
pour que celle-ci en le dupant s'acquière ses mérites. Inversement
la Sainte, quand le Mac la foule aux pieds, doit avoir conscience de
valoir plus que ce qui l'écrase: pour que le Mal soit parfait et

* Sartre, op. cit., p. 567.

l'injustice entière, il faut que le meilleur soit soumis au pire. Ainsi la Sainte sera supérieure dans son infériorité au criminel . . . comme sainte Blondine est supérieure aux bourreaux qui la tuent, et le criminel réduit à l'impuissance sera supérieur à la Sainte qui le trahit comme Samson aveuglé à Dalila.*

The Blacks,†for all its theatrical panache and the elaboration of its structure, does not do much more than re-echo the themes of *The Maids*. Whether one prefers the statement to be made with the classic economy of the latter or the romantic ebullience of the former is a matter of personal preference.

Genet, for more reasons than his sexual make-up, became the complete outsider, making continual war on the society which had thrown him out and which he hated accordingly. He is therefore peculiarly fitted to dramatise the outcast whether he is such by reason of character, class or race. He understands only too well that society's victims are what society makes them.

Pures émanations de leur maîtres les domestiques, comme les criminels, appartiennent à l'ordre de l'Autre, à l'ordre du Mal . . . basses, hypocrites, ingrates, méchantes parce que leurs patrons les rêvent telles . . . crées comme les Sudistes ont crée les nègres.‡

* 'Jean Genet, the weakest of all and the strongest' . . . Genet . . . refers to two opposing systems of values, . . . In the first the Pimp is destiny, pure Evil in its glamorous appearance; Genet is nothing but a dissolute hoodlum, just about good enough to be the slave of a rigorous master. In the second, Jean Genet, a cold, lucid consciousness, chains the criminal by his words, by his charms, leads him to destruction by honeyed betrayals. But each system implies the other . . . He (the criminal) must retain all of his superiority over the female Saint, so that the latter, in duping him acquires merits. Inversely, when the Pimp rides roughshod over her, the Saint must be conscious that she is of greater worth than that which crushes her: in order that Evil be perfect and justice entire, the best must be subjected to the worst. Thus, the Saint will be superior in her inferiority to the criminal . . . as St. Blondine is superior to the torturers who kill her and as the criminal who is reduced to impotence will be superior to the saint who betrays him, as the blinded Samson is superior to Delilah. Sartre, op. cit., p. 306, of French edition; pp. 329–36 of translation.

† Trans. B. Frechtman, Faber, 1960. First performed in Paris 1959.

‡ 'Le geste est sacré', Sartre, op. cit., p. 299.

To Genet the Negro has become an image of unique potency, for he hears him uttering more clearly than any other sufferers today the eternal cry: 'and if you wrong us shall we not revenge?'

> NEWPORT NEWS: As long as the earth revolves about the sun, which is itself carried off in a straight line to the very limits of God, in a secret chamber, Negroes will . . .
> BOBO: (*screaming*) Will hate! Yessir.
>
> <div align="right">(<i>The Blacks</i>, p. 66)</div>

His epigraph to his play is:

> One evening an actor asked me to write a play for an all-black cast. But what exactly is a black? First of all, what's his colour?

The black man thus becomes the representative of all who are exploited and oppressed for personal characteristics which are unacceptable to 'the compact majority', and Genet is able to voice their case with no less poignancy than do their own greatest writers. *The Blacks* might well be introduced by these words of James Baldwin:

> In the same way that we, for white people, were the descendants of Ham, and were cursed for ever, white people were, for us, the descendants of Cain. And the passion with which we loved the Lord was a measure of how deeply we feared and distrusted, and, in the end, hated almost all strangers, always, and avoided and despised ourselves. *

Genet, however, as was to be expected, goes further than this and emphasises the ambivalence of the love in hate felt by the slave for the master. Admitting that one Negro is capable of betraying another to their common oppressor, a Negress in the play declares she knows this to be so because

> of what goes on in my soul and what I call the temptation of the Whites.
>
> (p. 21)

* *The Fire Next Time*, James Baldwin, Michael Joseph, 1963.

Such a mixed emotion is felt by the killer himself, of whom another woman character can say:

> If I were sure he killed her in order to merge with the night . . .
> But I know he loved her.
>
> (p. 23)

In *The Blacks* Genet makes no overt use of the myth of the brothers, so although the play keeps us continually aware of the divided personalities which originate the violence of its action, it concerns us here principally because it uses, in extremely elaborate form a ritualisation of vengeance similar in artistic intention to that of the Elizabethan Revenge plays. There are four levels in the play and the last is a parallel to the 'mass' celebrated by Heironymo in his masque of *Perseda and Soleiman* or Titus in his grisly feast.* At the first level two Negroes kill an old white woman as part of a ritual murder, and another Negro, who betrays, or attempts to betray, them, is captured, tried by his fellows and summarily executed. All this takes place off stage and is ostensibly part of 'real life' since it is in order to distract the attention of the actual white audience from it that the black actors put on the play that takes place on the stage.

ARCHIBALD: Tonight our sole concern will be to entertain you.

(p. 18)

The entertainment consists of the story of a similar murder, played out before a stage audience mirroring the watching whites and acted by Negroes in white masks:

> This isn't a revival meeting, it is a ceremony,
>
> (p. 45)

declares Archibald, and the 'play within a play' of which he is the compère, is in fact a ritual mass, for its action revolves,

* v. supra, pp. 41–2.

sometimes literally, round a catafalque in which there is
in fact no body but which represents the sacrificed victim – in
this case a white woman, supposed to be killed by Village, a
young Negro, on the previous night. All is conducted according to a recognised rubric.

ARCHIBALD: You've no right to change anything in the ceremonial, unless, of course, you hit upon some cruel detail that
heightens it. . . . You're to obey me. And the text we've prepared.
(p. 17)

The play contains therefore a fourth recession since the
action which it commemorates is enacted with mime and dialogue, in the same way as in the early Christian drama the
events of Easter Sunday were enacted during the celebration
of the Easter mass. There is, of course, no attempt at naturalism.

ARCHIBALD: We shall increase the distance that separates us – a
distance that is basic – by our pomp, our manners, our insolence –
for we are also actors.

(p. 12)

In this ceremony there is no question of consecrating a sacred
wafer: the celebrants 'need a fresh corpse for every performance', and the voice of pity is equated with the voice of
squeamishness.

DIOUF: Actually we *could* use the same corpse a number of times.
It's presence is the thing that counts.

ARCHIBALD: What about the smell, Mr. Vicar-General?

(p. 18)

Like the two maids, the participants can only achieve their
purposes whether imagined as actual or as symbolic, when
they are 'there', and they pass the lead between them as the
improvisations are tossed between the members of a jazz *en-
semble*. 'It's dawn. Take it Absolom' cries an old woman, and
later Village approaches his climax in an ecstatic dance.

VILLAGE: (*dancing in front of the coffin*) . . . Now that she's dead, do you want me to open the coffin and repeat what I did with her when she was alive? You realise I'm supposed to re-enact it. . . .

FELICITY: Bring in the implements.

(*Bobo brings from behind the right screen a console-table on which are lying a blonde wig, a crude cardboard carnival mask representing a laughing white woman with big cheeks, a piece of pink knitting, two balls of wool, a knitting needle and white gloves.*)

(p. 43)

The transvestism in the following scene, in which the part of the white woman is played by the gentle Diouf, adds to the erotic tension but is actually irrelevant to the principal theme, although enforcing the underlying dichotomies which motivate the action.

The end of the 'mass' or 'masque' is followed by the death of all the 'whites' stage characters, and this recalls the fate of the spectators of Heironymo's play or Hamlet's duel, but the artistic distance is maintained. At the end the Governor, the Judge, the Missionary and the Valet fall on top of one another to the orchestrated laughter and cries of the Negroes until they rise to be shepherded off to hell by the Queen.

ARCHIBALD: Just a moment. The performance is coming to an end and we are about to disappear . . . The time has not yet come for presenting dramas about noble matters. But perhaps they suspect what lies behind this architecture of emptiness and words. We are what they want us to be. We shall therefore be it to the end, absurdly. Put your masks on again before leaving. Have them escorted to Hell.

(p. 95)

Thus although the significant murders are veiled by the stage devices of costume, dance, song and impersonation Genet transcends *A Spanish Tragedy* and its immediate successors in the elaboration of his stylised patterns. The central catafalque is a cloth thrown across two empty chairs, and whether or not we are asked to imagine that any death has 'actually' taken place may be unimportant and is certainly left slightly obscured by reference and innuendo. Nevertheless no artistic statement of the conflicts which stem from the ambivalence of Love-Hatred could be clearer or more horrific than that of this play.

The peculiar moral tension of Genet's apparent amoralism is made plain by a comparison of his work with the more truly nihilistic attitudes of some of his immediate predecessors. These are satirised by Bertold Brecht in his early play, *Baal*,* (1918) whose hero has been described as ' "A beatnik" of genius, a link between Rimbaud and Genet.' † This character commits Cain's sin and suffers Cain's punishment, but he never experiences Cain's guilt. Brecht is ridiculing the world of a decadent individualism from which all moral values had been discarded, and from the vacuum thus created he himself turned to the moral order of Marxism, which informs his later plays. In *Baal*, however, he contents himself with presenting a perjorative but not grossly distorted reflection of contemporary 'avant-gardisme'. Here he saw morality not inverted, as it is in Genet's plays, but abandoned as irrelevant to a creature so limited as man.

BAAL *sings*: The dearest place on earth was not (he'd say)
　　The grassy plot where his dead parents lay:

　　Nor a confessional nor harlot's bed
　　Nor a soft lap, warm, white, and fat (he said)

　　The place which he liked best to look upon
　　In this wide world of ours was the john . . .

　　A place where one can rest and yet where one
　　Gently but firmly can get business done.

Later, continuing the same vein of imagery, Baal remarks:

　　　　I see the world in a mellow light:
　　　　it is the Lord God's excrement.

* Included in *An Anthology of German Expressionist Drama*, Doubleday, 1963.　　　　† W. H. Sokel, Introduction to above.

In this mellowly lit world, Baal commits his brother-murder in an apparently casual fit of jealousy.

BAAL: Are you my friend, Ekhart. . . .

(*Ekhart, the waitress on his lap, laboriously gets up and tries to free his neck of her arm.*)

EKHART: What's the matter with you? It's nothing. Ridiculous.

(*Baal crouches to jump at him.*)

You won't be jealous of her? . . . Why shouldn't I have women? . . . Am I your lover?

(*Baal throws himself at him. . . .*)

WAITRESS: He's murdering him. Jesus! . . .

(*Baal gets up. Dusk falls suddenly. The lamp goes out.*)

BAAL: Ekhart!

After the killing Baal goes into his exile:

BAAL: The pale wind in the black trees . . . This is a small forest. I've been running on thick soles ever since I've been alone again in my skin. I must keep on bearing north. Follow the under-side of the leaves. I must leave that little affair behind me.

In the forest he finds temporary shelter in a woodmen's hut but soon the men go off to work as usual, leaving him to die alone.

BAAL: Mother! Ekhart should go away! . . .I want to go outside . . . It must be lighter out there. My dear Baal, you'll get to the door. You still have knees.

(*He crawls on all fours to the threshold.*)

Stars . . . Hm. (*He crawls out.*)

So dies the last romantic Cain—unpitied and uncondemned by his creator, and equally unapproved. In a world which is the excrement of God, good and evil, love and hatred are not only

without value but—more important—are without any particular interest. The primordial murder here does not even
excite disgust. Against this vision of mankind, which—it must
be repeated—is not Brecht's own but that of those he considers man's enemies, Genet's urgent concern with love and
hatred, his anger at exploitation of the weak and the despera-
tion of his search, however vain, for a hope of succour, shine
with a brightness equal to the *expertise* of their dramatisation.

CHAPTER 7

THE DISAPPEARANCE OF THE IMAGE
IN ENGLAND AND AMERICA

O Balin, O Balan!
how blood you both
the *Brudersee*
towards the last phase
of our dear West,
D. JONES, *Anathemata*

IN *A Sleep of Prisoners*,* by Christopher Fry, the modern
theatre sees the story of Cain and Abel dramatised once more
in something approaching its original form. In fact Fry is even
closer to the Christian typology than are the medieval plays,
for he indicates more forcibly the role of Abel as the prototype
of the Redeemer. Private Peter Able, the Abel of the dream-
sequence, is the holy fool, who is loved and hated by his
brother, whose loves and hates he refuses to share, and who
reveals the way which would lead to salvation, if humanity
were not too frightened to walk in it. This fear of the un-
known drives David King to trust only his animal responses to
his material environment, and he resents the dichotomy of his
own nature which makes him 'Like a half-wit angel strapped
to the back of a mule.'

> DAVID: Amply, the animal is Cain, thank God
> As he was meant to be: a huskular strapling
> With all his passions about him.   (p. 13)

Peter, however, will not accept the horrors involved in physical existence without knowledge of their justification.

> PETER: . . . Other lives, forbear
> To blame me, great and small forgive me

* Oxford, 1951.

> If to your various agonies
> My light should seem hardly enough
> To be the cause of the ponderable shadow.

(p. 17)

David challenges him first to a game:

> We'll put it to the High and Mighty.
> Play you dice to know who's favoured.

In action the dicing is heightened until it becomes a stylised image of violent conflict, during which the sons are watched by their father.

> ADAMS: Look, sir, my sons are playing,
>   How silent the spectators are,
>   World, air and water. . . . .
>   Cain's your man.
>   He goes in the mould of passion as you made him.
>   . . . The other boy
>   Frets for what never came his way,
>   Will never reconcile us to our exile. . . .
>   Cain sweats: Cain gleams. Now do you see him?
>   He gives his body to the game.

But David is throwing 'by twos and threes'; Peter is winning.

> PETER: Deal me high, deal me low.
>   Make my deeds
>   My nameless needs.
>   I know I do not know
>   . . . That brings me home!
>
> *David roars with rage and disappointment.*

Peter cries: 'It was a game between us, Cain', but David cannot endure the sense of his own inferiority:

> DAVID: You leave us now, leave us, you half and half:
>   I want to be free of you.

Their father, watching the fight, is powerless to intervene for
his sons are the two equal sides of himself:

> ADAMS: I made them both, the fury and the suffering,
>   The fury, the suffering, the two ways
>   Which here spreadeagle me.

The dream voice of God is heard; Cain understands too late
something of his loss and of his error.

> MEADOWS: Cain; I hear your brother's blood
>   Crying to me from the ground.
> DAVID: Sir, no; he is silent.
>   All the crying is mine. . . .
>   How was I expected to guess
>   That what I am you didn't want?

(pp. 13–19)

Within the limitations of a simple framework the play presents
in genuinely theatrical form the author's contention that: 'The
enterprise is exploration unto God', and it makes of the brother-
murder a viable image of man's divided attitude towards such
a demand on his too limited personal resources.

Like Fry, Archibald Macleish has retained the Biblical
names and settings in his play *Nobodaddy*.* He has, however,
attempted to catch his audience's response by reversing the
roles of the brothers and creating a gnostic Cain who asserts
his freedom by his rebellion against Abel's blood-sacrifice and
proclaims his own superiority as a cultivator of the soil.

> CAIN: (*To Abel*) Because you fear
>   Must I fear too? Because you are a thing
>   Of earth and water must I likewise be
>   Water and earth? You are that root of me
>   That ties itself far down in the old slime
>   From which he took us. But I will not have
>   Roots in the earth. I am a man to walk—
>   Take off your hands from me.

* Dunster House, Cambridge, 1926.

The thought is not uninteresting, but the play is a closet drama without much theatrical or literary importance.

In *Serjeant Musgrave's Dance** John Arden has written a play in the direct line of succession from the Elizabethan Revenge drama. On its first production the play received an unusually varied reception, but even the most hostile critics agreed on the power of the penultimate scene, and this is a point where the old convention can be observed working its magic yet once again. When Musgrave reveals the skeleton of Private Billy Hicks hanging on the lamp-bracket, and when he dances his fantastic jig before the horrified spectators, he is repeating the role of old Heironymo, who three centuries earlier had pulled back the curtain to reveal his son's body and cried:

Here was my son, and here my son lies dead.†

There is the same maniacal frenzy and also something of the same dramatic distance achieved by the convention of masque or dance. The passage must be allowed to speak for itself.

MUSGRAVE: ... D'ye hear me, d'ye hear me, d'ye hear me—
I'm the Queen of England's man, and I'm wearing her coat. ...
I'm Black Jack Musgrave, me, the hardest serjeant of the line. ...
Look—I'll show it to you all. And I'll *dance* for you beneath it—
hoist up the flag, boy—up, up, *up*!

(*Attercliffe has nipped up the ladder, holding the rope. He loops the rope over the cross-bar of the lamp-bracket, drops to the plinth again, flings open the lid of the big box, and hauls on the rope.*

Hurst beats frantically on his drum. The rope is attached to the contents of the box, and these are jerked up to the cross-bar and reveal themselves as an articulated skeleton dressed in a soldier's tunic and trousers, the rope noosed round the neck.

The people draw back in horror. Musgrave begins to dance, waving his rifle, his face contorted with demoniac fury.)

MUSGRAVE: (*as he dances, sings, with mounting emphasis*)
Up he goes and no one knows
How to bring him downwards

* Methuen, 1960.   † v. supra, p. 42.

Dead man's feet
Over the street
Riding the roofs
And crying down your chimneys
Up he goes and no one knows
Who it was that rose him
But white and red
He waves his head
He sits on your back
And you'll never lose him
Up he goes and no one knows
How to bring him downwards.

(*He breaks off at the climax of the song, and stands panting. The drum stops.*)

That'll do, that'll do for *that.* (*He beckons gently to the people.*) You can come back. Come back. Come back . . . Now I said I'll explain. So listen.

(pp. 84–5)

There follows, again in Kyd's own fashion, the long explanatory narrative. The young soldier, serving with an army of occupation, had been shot by terrorists, and the order had been given to bring in the assassins. They were not found, but in the search five other of the native inhabitants had been killed in their turn, and there seemed no end to the opening vista of murder and vengeance.

You were all for enlisting, it'd still have gone on,

as Musgrave told his crowd of English miners.

After his great denunciation of imperialistic violence, the serjeant 'sits down and broods'–a true replica of the melancholy avenger of tradition–and at last announces his fantastic and horrible plan.

One man, and for him five. Therefore, for five of them we multiply out, *and* we find it five-and-twenty . . . So, as I understand Logic and Logic to me is the mechanism of God–that means that today there's twenty-five persons will have to be–.

(p. 91)

Unlike Heironymo's, however, Musgrave's vengeance is prevented by the pacifism of one of his own supporters, the broken
love of a woman and the timely arrival of the dragoons.
Annie knows that to avenge her lover's death will never bring
him back to her:

> My true love is a scarecrow
> Of rotted rag and bone
> Ask him: where are the birds, Billy?
> Where have they all gone?

(p. 95)

Billy Hicks' skeleton was roused ghost-like from his coffin and
voiced once more the plea of the blood shed upon the ground,
but its voice was unheeded. What Musgrave sings below the
body of Billy Hicks raised high in the market-place, makes of
the victim as clear a type of the suffering saviour as medieval
exegesis made of Abel. But though he is lifted up, no man is
drawn unto him. No one supports Musgrave; the 'Establishment' is vindicated by force, and the Avenger must die. John
Arden has used the old images for the sake of their dramatic
power, but, like Chapman and Marston before him, he can no
longer relate them to his own society. In the prison cell,
Musgrave, his pacific comrade and his old landlady try once
more to fit the pieces of the puzzle together but leave it un-
solved in the end.

MUSGRAVE: Don't tell me there was life or love in this town.

MRS. HITCHCOCK: There was. There was hungry men, too—
fighting for their food. But *you* brought in a different war.

MUSGRAVE: I brought it in to end it.

ATTERCLIFFE: To end it by its own rules: no bloody good. She's
right, you're wrong. You can't cure the pox by further whor-
ing . . .

MUSGRAVE: That's not the truth. (*He looks at them both in appeal,
but they nod.*) That's not the truth. God was with me . . . God . . .
(*He makes a strange animal noise of despair, a sort of sob that is*

3. Cain and Abel: a model for the Political Prisoner.
By F. E. McWilliam, 1952.

choked off suddenly before it can develop into a full howl.)—and
all they dancing—all of them—there.

MRS. HITCHCOCK: Ah, not for long. And it's not a dance of joy.
Those men are hungry, so they've got no time for *you*. One day
they'll be full, though, and the Dragoons'll be gone, and then
they'll remember.

MUSGRAVE: (*shaking his head*) No.

MRS. HITCHCOCK: Let's hope it, any road. Eh?

*She presents the glass to his lips. This time he accepts it and drinks,
and remains silent.*

(pp. 102–3)

No other contemporary play uses the traditional material of
the brother-murder with the moral force that inspired *Serjeant Musgrave's Dance*. Although it re-appears in many
plays, this is for the sake of its psychological rather than its
ethical significance. In *Chips with Everything** Arnold Wesker
makes the destruction of one friend by the other the price paid
by Pip for his re-adoption into his old social cast. Returning
from the interview with his superiors in which he agrees to
become an officer cadet, Pip finds one of his unit waiting for
him in the empty hut. Tentatively Charles makes his stum-
bling advances:

CHARLES: You see—you know me, don't you, you know the sort
of bloke . . . I'm—I'm, I'm not dumb, I'm not a fool, I'm not a
real fool, not a bloody moron and I thought, well, I thought
maybe you could teach me—something, Eh? Well, not anything
but something proper, real.

Pip refuses to hear him, and Charles' new-won confidence
begins to fade.

I can't read books but I can listen to you. Maybe we'll get posted
to the same place, and then every evening, every other evening,
or once a week, even, you could talk to me for a bit, for half an
hour say.

* Penguin Books, 1963.

N

But the other man, who has already signed away his inde-
pendence, dares not respond.

PIP: Someone else, Charles, not me, someone else.

CHARLES: There you go. You're a hypocrite–a hypocrite you are.
You take people to the edge. Don't you know what I'm asking
you? don't you know what I'm really asking you? . . . Ask someone else. The truth is you're scared aren't you? You call us mate,
but you're a scared old schoolboy. The pilot officer was right,
you're slumming. You're a bleeding slummer.

Pip, since he is committed elsewhere, is driven on to destroy
their relationship and resists Charles' last plea as ruthlessly
as his first:

CHARLES: I'll do what *you* want, Pip.

PIP: Swop masters? You're a fool, Charles, the kind of fool my
fathers fed on, you're a fool, a fool . . .

(pp. 64–8)

His adolescent egalitarianism has failed Pip, and the betrayal
of his new working-class comrade reflects the betrayal of the
crusade for social justice upon which he had set out so con-
fidently.

In the last group of plays to be reviewed the personal
relationship of the brothers and their individual fates become
the dramatists' primary concern. In Eugene O'Neill's masterpiece, his autobiographical play, *Long Day's Journey Into
Night,** the relationship between Jamie and Edmund is a
comparatively unimportant thread in the fabric, but the
revelation of the love-hatred of the elder brother for the
younger in the last act of the play is unsurpassed in modern
drama for its perceptiveness and power. In the night following
the day on which their mother relapses into her drug addiction,
and Edmund is told he is suffering from tuberculosis, the elder
brother comes home drunk.

* Jonathan Cape. Written in 1940; first published in Great Britain 1956.

JAMIE: . . . . Listen, Kid, you'll be going away. May not get another chance to talk. Or might not be drunk enough to tell you the truth. So got to tell you now . . . Want to warn you—against me. Mama and Papa are right. I've been rotten bad influence. And worst of it is, I did it on purpose.

EDMUND: Shut up! I don't want to hear—

JAMIE: Nix, Kid! You listen! Did it on purpose to make a bum of you. Or part of me did. A big part. That part that's been dead so long. That hates life. My putting you wise so you'd learn from my mistakes. Believed that myself at times, but it's a fake. Made my mistakes look good. Made getting drunk romantic. Made whores fascinating vampires instead of the poor, stupid, diseased slobs they really are. Made fun of work as sucker's game. Never wanted you to succeed and make me look even worse by comparison. Wanted you to fail. Always jealous of you. Mama's baby, Papa's pet! And it was your being born that started Mama on dope. I know that's not your fault, but all the same, God damn you, I can't help hating your guts—!

EDMUND: Jamie! Cut it out! You're crazy!

JAMIE: But don't get wrong idea, Kid. I love you more than I hate you. My saying what I'm telling you now proves it. I run the risk you'll hate me—and you're all I've got left. But I didn't mean to tell you that last stuff—go that far back. Don't know what made me. What I wanted to say is, I'd like to see you become the greatest success in the world. But you'd better be on your guard. Because I'll do my damnedest to make you fail. Can't help it. I hate myself. Got to take revenge. On everyone else. Especially you. Oscar Wilde's 'Reading Gaol' has the dope twisted. The man was dead, and so he had to kill the thing he loved. That's what it ought to be. The dead part of me hopes you won't get well. Maybe he's even glad the game has got Mama again! He wants company, he doesn't want to be the only corpse around the house.

EDMUND: Jesus, Jamie! You really have gone crazy!

JAMIE: Think it over and you'll see I'm right. Think it over when you're away from me in the sanatorium. Make up your mind you've got to tie a can to me—get me out of your life—think of me as dead—tell people, 'I had a brother, but he's dead.' And when you come back, look out for me. I'll be waiting to welcome you with that 'my old pal' stuff, and give you the glad hand, and at the first good chance I get stab you in the back.

EDMUND: Shut up! I'll be God-damned if I'll listen to you any more–!

JAMIE: Only don't forget me. Remember I warned you–for your sake. Give me credit. Greater love hath no man than this, that he saveth his brother from himself.

(pp. 145–7)

This dialogue does not advance the action of the play, nor are any conclusions drawn from it; it must simply be appreciated for what it is and for what it reveals of the working of a man's mind.

It is in tune with the preoccupations of the third quarter of the twentieth century that the story of the brother-murder should be related to homosexual love. Among the earliest plays to do this explicitly is *South* by Julian Greene.* Here the setting of the story at the start of the American Civil War serves merely as a frame for the portrait of Ian Cheveesky, a Polish lieutenant, staying on a Southern plantation. His sexual inversion is recognised by no one except himself and the woman who loves him, and the climax of the play is the silent moment when he 'falls in love at first sight' with a young planter, MacClure, who is courting his host's daughter. Any relationship between the two men is prevented by the guilty misery of the one and the unawareness of the other, and 'They stare at one another, each waiting for the other to volunteer to do what both wish but are not able to do'.† It is the frustration which he faces that exposes the inversion of Cheveesky's passion. Alone with MacClure he analyses the situation and faces what is, to him, its inevitable conclusion.

IAN: Something else is breaking my heart, something that you can't understand, and what I read in your face is the invincible

* In *Plays of the Year*, 1954–5, Elek.
† Martin Buber's translation of a single Fuegian word, meaning 'far away', op. cit., p. 18.

ignorance of the pure in heart where the suffering of the world is concerned. You have never loved, Eric MacClure.

. . . A word would be enough to open your eyes, but that very word, which I won't speak, would seem more mysterious and more abominable to you than all the rest.

(pp. 185–17)

What are you doing here, alone in this room with me talking of love? . . (*He seizes his arm and pushes him in front of the mirror*) . . . look at yourself! It's you that are enclosed in a ban, in a circle of horror. It surrounds your face, your shoulders, your hands. Look at that brow, innocent of all desire, those lips that no lips have ever touched because you're afraid and spread that fear around you.

MACCLURE: Let me go! If you want to fight we can go outside, but you're mad to pick a quarrel with me. I wish you no harm.

IAN: I'm not picking a quarrel with you, you fool! I want to kill you.

(p. 190)

The duel which Ian provokes and in which he loses his life is described by his second, who does not realise the sexual implication of his words:

MR. WHITE: It was the hand of God . . . The lieutenant scarcely defended himself. Perhaps a little at first, but towards the end his face changed. You felt he was offered like a victim to the fury he had unleashed. MacClure was terrible—he struck and struck, again and again. He was like a destroying angel. The last blow was struck at the head, the whole face. Lieutenant Cheveesky collapsed as though he'd been felled.

The young man attempts to justify himself as a righteous avenger after the old pattern:

MACCLURE: Didn't he himself put the sword in the hand that struck him down? . . . . God allowed all this to happen.

But such an interpretation is denied by the more sympathetic old planter:

BRODERICK: Don't bring God into a murder, don't make Him your accomplice. If He is the way you imagine Him, what a horrible God He is.

MacClure is nearer the truth when he says:

He wanted to die. He wanted it with all his might. I realised it too late.   (pp. 200 ff.)

The ambivalence at the heart of every 'I–Thou' relationship is likely to be particularly marked in homosexual love. In this case the warring brothers have changed roles: the passive recipient of love has become active, and the original Cain receives passively the death he had planned for Abel since only so can he experience assuagement. The duel becomes the image of the psychological *impasse*. The play is unconcerned with the sins of either aggression or sensuality, and it has no truck with considerations of guilt or justice. It demands from its audience only the response of pity.

In *The Collection** by Harold Pinter, the figure of Cain is divided between two men. The victim, Bill, is a young homosexual living under the protection of Harry, an older man. He is accused by their neighbour, James Horne, an insensitive narcissist, of seducing his wife. Bill, unsure of himself and flattered perhaps by this tribute to his virility, does not deny the accusation, and an ambivalent relationship develops between the two men, until Horne feels strong enough to change from verbal to physical warfare. He picks up a fruit knife and runs his finger along the edge.

JAMES: This is fairly sharp.

BILL: What do you mean?

JAMES: Come on.

* Methuen, 1962.

BILL: I beg your pardon?

JAMES: Come on. You've got that one. I've got this one.

BILL: What about it?

JAMES: I get a bit tired of words sometimes, don't you? Let's have a game. For fun.

BILL: What sort of game?

JAMES: Let's have a mock duel.

BILL: I don't want a mock duel, thank you.

JAMES: Of course you do. Come on. First one who's touched is a sissy.

BILL: This is rather unsubtle, don't you think?

JAMES: Not in the least. Come on, into first position.

BILL: I thought we were friends.

JAMES: Of course we're friends. What on earth's the matter with you? I'm not going to kill you. It's just a game, that's all. We're playing a game. You're not windy, are you?

BILL: I think it's silly.

JAMES: I say, you're a bit of a spoilsport, aren't you?

BILL: I'm putting my knife down anyway.

JAMES: Well, I'll pick it up.

(*James does so and faces him with two knives.*)

BILL: Now you've got two.

JAMES: I've got another one in my hip pocket.

BILL: What do you do, swallow them?

JAMES: Do you?

(*They stare at each other.*)

Go on! Swallow it!

(*James throws a knife at Bill's face. Bill throws up a hand to protect his face and catches the knife by the blade. It cuts his hand.*)

BILL: Ow!

JAMES: Well caught! What's the matter? Let's have a look. Ah yes. Now you've got a scar on your hand. You didn't have one before, did you?

(pp. 39–41)

It is, however, the older man who finally destroys Bill, and the cruelty of his attack brands him inexorably with the mark of the 'eldest primal curse'. Ignoring his friend sitting hunched and silent, he addresses James:

HARRY: Bill's a slum boy, you see, he's got a slum sense of humour. That's why I never take him along with me to parties. Because he's got a slum mind. I have nothing against slum minds *per se*, you understand, nothing at all. There's a certain kind of slum mind which is perfectly all right in a slum, but when this kind of slum mind gets out of the slum it sometimes persists, you see, it rots everything. That's what Bill is. There's something faintly putrid about him, don't you find? Like a slug. There's nothing wrong with slugs in their place, but he's a slum slug; there's nothing wrong with slum slugs in their place, but this one won't keep his place—he crawls all over the walls of nice houses leaving slime, don't you boy? He confirms stupid sordid little stories just to amuse himself, while everyone else has to run round in circles to get to the root of the matter and smooth the whole thing out. All he can do is sit and suck his bloody hand and decompose like the filthy putrid slum slug he is. What about another whisky, Horne?

(pp. 42–3)

Bill is broken at last and driven to confess his impotence:

BILL: I'll . . . tell you . . . the truth.

HARRY: Oh, for God's sake, don't be ridiculous. Come on Mr. Horne, off you go now, back to your wife, old boy, leave this . . . tyke to me.

(*James does not move.*)

Come on, Jimmy, I think we've had enough of this stupidity, don't you?

(James looks at him sharply. Harry stops still.)

BILL: I never touched her . . . we sat . . . in the lounge, on a sofa . . . for two hours . . . talked . . . we talked about it . . . we didn't . . . move from the lounge . . . never went to her room . . . just talked . . . about what we would do . . . if we did get to her room . . . two hours . . . we never touched . . . we just talked about it . . .

(Long silence. James leaves the house. Harry sits. Bill remains sucking his hand. Silence.)

(pp. 44–5)

For this 'Abel', as for this 'Cain', there is offered no hope of either vengeance or redemption, and the word justice has become a sound without meaning. Victim and executioner are what they are and do what they must; comment is useless, judgement an insult, and pity is perhaps considered irrelevant.

The last play to be considered in this group is *Zoo Story* * by the American, Edward Albee. Here, as in *South*, the myth is twisted, for the aggressor throws down the knife at his victim's feet, and himself by 'a moment of complete surrender,/ Costing not less than everything'† achieves before death a transient fulfilment and peace. Jerry finds Peter sitting on a bench in the park and, in Ancient Mariner fashion, forces him to listen to his story. It concerns his desperate attempt to come to terms with his landlady's mongrel dog, first by being friendly towards him, and then, when the animal persists in attacking him, by poisoning the creature. Even in this he fails, for the dog recovers and faces him once more in the hallway.

JERRY: I think we stayed a long time that way . . . still, stone-statues . . . just looking at one another. I looked more into his face than he looked into mine. I mean I can concentrate longer at looking into a dog's face than a dog can concentrate at looking into mine, or into anybody else's face, for that matter. But during

* Jonathan Cape, 1962.
† T. S. Eliot, 'Little Gidding', *Four Quartets*, Faber & Faber, 1944.

that twenty seconds or two hours that we looked into each other's face, we made contact. Now, here is what I had wanted to happen: I loved that dog now, and I wanted him to love me. I had tried to love, and I had tried to kill, and both had been unsuccessful by themselves. I hoped . . . and I don't really know why I expected the dog to understand anything, much less my motivations . . . I hoped that the dog would understand. It's just . . . it's just that . . . it's just that if you can't deal with people you have to make a start somewhere. WITH ANIMALS! Don't you see? A person has to have some way of dealing with SOMETHING. If not with people . . . SOMETHING. With a bed, with a cockroach, with a mirror . . . no, that's too hard, that's one of the last steps.

(pp. 130–1)

His listener, who up to this point in his life, has believed himself a socially integrated and contented individual, recognises without admitting it the isolation of what Jerry has called 'the permanent transient'. Knowing his hearer understands him, Jerry moves in to his climax.

JERRY: And what has been the result: the dog and I have attained a compromise: more of a bargain, really. We neither love nor hurt because we do not try to reach each other. And, *was* trying to feed the dog an act of love? And, perhaps, was the dog's attempt to bite me *not* an act of love? If we can so misunderstand, well then, why have we invented the word love in the first place?

(*There is silence. Jerry moves to Peter's bench and sits down beside him.*)

The Story of Jerry and the Dog: the end . . .

PETER: (*numb*) I . . . I don't understand what . . . I don't think I . . . (*now almost tearfully*). Why did you tell me all of this?

JERRY: Why not?

PETER: I DON'T UNDERSTAND!

JERRY: (*furious, but whispering*) That's a lie.

(pp. 132–3)

Jerry now attempts to establish contact with Peter, whom he

has recognised as one of his own kind, by means of aggression; he pushes him off the park bench and goads him to fight, finally throwing him his own knife.

JERRY: Now you pick up that knife and you fight with me. You fight for your self-respect; you fight for that god-damned bench.

PETER: (*struggling*) No! Let . . . let go of me! He . . . Help!

JERRY: (*slaps Peter on each 'fight'*) You fight, you miserable bastard; fight for that bench; fight for your parakeets; fight for your cats; fight for your two daughters; fight for your wife; fight for your manhood, you pathetic little vegetable. (*Spits in Peter's face.*) You couldn't even get your wife with a male child. . . .

At last Peter picks up the knife.

(*Peter holds the knife with a firm arm, but far in front of him, not to attack, but to defend.*)

JERRY: (*sighs heavily*) So be it!

(*With a rush he charges Peter and impales himself on the knife. For just a moment, complete silence.*)

(p. 140)

'Relation is mutual . . . I become through my relation to the Thou; as I become *I*, I say *Thou*. All real living is meeting.' * Jerry accepts the price which even a fleeting moment of such living may exact. In death is found momentarily contact and love.

JERRY: Oh, Peter, I was so afraid I'd drive you away. (*He laughs as best he can.*) You don't know how afraid I was you'd go away and leave me. And now I'll tell you what happened at the zoo . . . I think . . . I think that while I was at the zoo I decided that I would walk north . . . until I found you . . . or somebody . . . and I decided that I would talk to you . . . I would tell you things . . . and things that I would tell you would . . . Well, here we are. You see? Here we *are* . . . Peter . . . Peter? . . . Peter

* Martin Buber, *I and Thou*, pp. 8 and 11.

... thank you. I came unto you (*he laughs, so faintly*) and you have comforted me. Dear Peter.

(p. 141)

He has proved at least to himself, that the word love has not 'just been invented', but in the world as it has been created for men, love can, it seems, be discovered only in death.

In Albee's play, *Who's Afraid of Virginia Woolf?** the warring pair, a husband and wife, are mutually destructive. The woman is the original aggressor, but it is she who is, at last, completely destroyed. The warfare is entirely verbal, but the intensity of passion as each strips the other 'to the buff— buff for buffalo'† is surpassed in the violence of its brutality only, perhaps, in the plays of Jean Genet. It is the husband who discovers and uses the weapon which breaks the apparently unbreakable clinch. He deliberately violates their shared fantasy, by destroying the image of the child they never had, an image which Martha had cherished for twenty years.

GEORGE: Martha . . . our son is dead . . . He was killed . . . late in the afternoon . . . on a country road, with his learner's permit in his pocket, he swerved to avoid a porcupine, and drove straight into . . .

MARTHA: YOU CAN'T . . . DO . . . THAT!

GEORGE: . . . large tree . . .

MARTHA: YOU CANNOT DO THAT . . .

GEORGE: I can kill him, Martha, if I want to . . .

MARTHA: HE IS OUR CHILD.

GEORGE: AND I HAVE KILLED HIM.

MARTHA: NO.

GEORGE: YES . . .

Requiem aeternam dona eis, Domine.

---

* Jonathan Cape, 1964.
† Beckett, *All That Fall*, Faber & Faber, 1957.

Martha's surrender, when it comes, is abject and complete:

MARTHA: I'm cold.

GEORGE: It's late.

MARTHA: Yes.

GEORGE: Are you all right?

MARTHA: Yes. No.

GEORGE: (*very softly*) . . .
Who's afraid of Virginia Woolf
Virginia Woolf
Virginia . . .

MARTHA: I . . . am . . . George.

GEORGE: Who's afraid of Virginia Woolf . . .

MARTHA: I . . . am . . . George . . . I . . . am.

The knowledge of such a weapon and the realisation that its use would be mortal might seem to belong by right to a post-Freudian generation, but in fact Henrik Ibsen, that intuitive but ruthless psychologist, had discovered it almost exactly a century before Albee's play was written. When Brand kills his wife—literally in this case—it is by his demand for the sacrifice not of their son but of the phantasm that haunted the mother's mind after the baby was lost, and that crept up from the graveyard to watch the Christmas candles through the window. When Brand destroys this image by his demand that the baby-clothes on which Agnes fed her fantasy be given to the beggar-woman, Agnes died.

CHAPTER 8

'AMÉDÉE OR HOW TO GET RID OF IT'

Remove away that black'ning church:
Remove away that marriage hearse:
Remove away that man of blood
You'll quite remove the ancient curse.

W. BLAKE, *A Little Boy Lost*

THE theatre of Western Europe and America has shown itself
sensitive to the story of the 'Two Brothers' in the Semitic and
Aryan forms of the myth. It has been, that is to say, consistently concerned with the concepts of a primordial sin followed by guilt and, until very recently, with its punishment.
The plays move in a world of Good and Evil, where, according
to Jung, the perfection of the Christian Trinity is maintained
by the casting out of the fourth element to wander as Cain or
as Satan in unending exile from God.* These brothers are not
like the Dioscuri of the Greeks, who both spend alternate days
in the kingdom of light and of darkness,† nor do they represent the dual principles of reason and emotion, the male and
female principles, which receive their triumphant dramatisation in *The Bacchae*. Their story is concerned essentially with a
sin and its consequences. But European man's faith in the
possibility of individual responsibility and moral judgement
has weakened. As the traditional authorities of Church and
State have declined, and the imposed authorities of the new
dictatorships offer less of hope to thinking men, the significance of the fighting twins, as reflected in creative work,
becomes both more varied and more obscure. Obligations
appear to remain, but judgement of the failure to fulfil the

* V. Jung, *Psychology and Religion: West and East*, Collected Works XI,
Routledge and Kegan Paul, 1958, pp. 59, 63, 391.

† V. Kerenyi, *The Gods of the Greeks*, Thames & Hudson, 1951;
Pelican Books, p. 108.

obligations becomes impossible. Moreover men feel themselves ever less able to establish sufficient communication with their fellows to know what obligations and failures are involved in their inter-relationships.

Can the cycle be broken? Can the falcon 'in the widening gyre'* ever hope again to hear the falconer? This last chapter can adumbrate only two faint hopes. The first lies in such compassion and foresight as inspires a poem by John Wain, 'On the Death of a Murderer'.†

'One day Vera showed us a photograph of some local Gestapo men; . . . . they stared out at us with professionally menacing but unhappy eyes . . . After the relief of Prague those young men were hunted through the countryside . . . . like wild game and all of them were taken and killed.'

(E. MUIR, Autobiography)

> Over the hill the city lights leap up.
> But here in the fields the quiet dusk folds down.
> A man lies in a ditch. He listens hard . . . .
> They are coming, and he can run no further . . .
> He will die.
> They have taken away his whip and gun. . . .
> He will die, this cursed man. The first pursuer
> Is here. The darkness is ready to give him up
> He has, at most, a hundred breaths to draw . . . .
> The man's body will rot under lime, and that soon.
> But the parades have taught his uniform to march.
> The hunters close in: do they feel the danger?
> When they wrench his body to pieces, will they hear
> A sigh as his spirit is sucked into the air
> That they must breathe? . . . .
> And who shall save them
> If after all the years and all the deaths
> They find a world still pitiless, a street
> Where no grass of love grows over the hard stones?

But Cain does not only need to be forgiven, he needs also

* W. B. Yeats, 'The Second Coming', *Collected Poems*, Macmillan, 1933, p. 210.

† From *Weep before God!*, Macmillan, 1961.

the strength to forgive himself. Too many are like 'that old beggar', told of by the judge-penitent of *The Fall** who wouldn't let go of his hand one day. ' "Oh sir," he said, "it's not just that I am no good, but you lose track of the light." Yes, we have lost track of the light, the mornings, the holy innocence of those who forgive themselves.'

One of the most poignant theatrical images of this dual need is the encounter between Son and Father in Eugene Ionesco's *Victims of Duty*.† The two figures are sitting opposite each other but can neither hear nor see each other. The father is, presumably, dead, the son, deep in his recovered memories of boyhood.

CHOUBERT: Father, we never understood each other . . . Can you still hear me? I'll be obedient; forgive us as we forgave you . . . You used to hit me. But I was stronger than you. My contempt hit you much harder. That was what killed you. Wasn't it? Listen . . . I had to avenge my mother . . . I *had* to . . . What *was* my duty? . . . Did I really *have* to? . . . She forgave you, but I went on and carried out *her* revenge myself . . . What's the good of taking vengeance? It's always the avenger who suffers . . . What right had I to punish you? Let's make it up! Let's be friends! . . . . You don't want to . . . If you would look at me, you'd see how alike we are. I've all the same faults as you. (*Silence* . . .) Who will have mercy on me, I who have been unmerciful! Even if you did forgive me, I could never forgive myself!

(p. 286)

The father, remembering the hope and anguish with which he had contemplated the birth of his son, voices the recurrent disillusion of the parent, but the son hears nothing.

DETECTIVE'S VOICE: (*speaking as the father*) . . . I had forgiven the world, for love of you. Everything was saved, because now nothing could ever wipe out the fact of your birth into the living universe. Even when you are no more, I told myself, nothing can alter the fact that you *have been*. You were here, for ever inscribed in the archives of the universe, firmly fixed in the eternal

* Op. cit., p. 106.   † *Plays*, II, John Calder, 1958.

memory of God . . . And you . . . The more proud I was of you, the more I loved you, the more you despised me, accused me of every crime, some I had committed, others I had not. Then there was your mother, poor soul. But who can tell what passed between us, whether it was her fault, or my fault, her fault or my fault . . .

CHOUBERT: He'll never speak again, and it's all my fault, my fault! . . . .

DETECTIVE'S VOICE: You can reject me and blush for me and insult my memory as much as you like. I'll not blame you. I'm no longer capable of hate. I can't help forgiving. I owe you more than you owe me. I wouldn't want you to suffer, I want you to stop feeling guilty. Forget what you consider to be my faults.

CHOUBERT: Father, why don't you speak, why don't you answer me! . . . How sad to think that never, never again I shall hear your voice. Never, never, never, never . . . And I shall never know . . .

(pp. 288–9)

The dilemma appears absolute; the *impasse* unbreakable, but from this point Ionesco takes that further leap forward which is so rarely achieved, even in the imaginative world of the artist. His play *Amédée, or How to Get Rid of It,** begins as a fantastic modern parallel to the primordial myth. The murder with which the play deals is obscure, but it is presumably some form of the murder of love, although the first signs of it are not blood spots but fungi.

AMÉDÉE: A mushroom! Well, really! If they're going to start growing in the dining-room! . . . It's the last straw! . . . Poisonous, of course!

(p. 154)

These are the play's opening lines. The growth of the mushrooms is associated with the presence of a corpse in the bedroom, a corpse horrifying and yet fascinating to both Amédée and his wife, Madeleine.

* *Plays*, II, John Calder, 1958.

O

MADELEINE: . . . Now *you're* looking at him! . . . I get blamed if *I* do it . . . *Will* you shut that door! . . .

AMÉDÉE: I was only looking to see if he'd grown! . . . You'd almost think he had, a little.

MADELEINE: Not since yesterday . . . or at least not that you'd notice!

AMÉDÉE: It may be all over, you know. Perhaps he's stopped.

(p. 157)

But the power of the victim over his murderers only increases with time. A little later, while his wife busies herself with incomprehensible trivialities, Amédée tip-toes again to the bluebeard's chamber.

MADELEINE: You were watching him . . .

AMÉDÉE: I couldn't help myself . . .

MADELEINE: It won't do any good, it won't *help* . . .

AMÉDÉE: He's grown again. Soon, the divan won't be big enough for him. His feet are over the end already. I seem to remember fifteen years ago he was rather short. And so young. Now he's got a great white beard . . .

(p. 164)

The emergence of the hidden guilt into the everyday world as the corpse grows is a grotesquely funny theatrical image which is also in its implications potentially tragic.

(*Suddenly, from the adjoining room, a violent bang is heard against the wall . . .*)

MADELEINE: Ah!

AMÉDÉE: Keep calm, keep calm!

(*The left-hand door gradually gives way, as though under steady pressure.*)

MADELEINE: Ah! Heaven help us!

(*Then Amédée and Madeleine, dumb with terror, watch two*

*enormous feet slide slowly in through the open door and advance
about eighteen inches onto the stage.)*

MADELEINE: Look!

AMÉDÉE: I'm looking. (*He rushes forward, lifts the feet and sets
them carefully on a stool or chair.*)
Well, that's the limit!

MADELEINE: What's he doing to us now? What does he want? . . .

AMÉDÉE: I'll go and fold him up . . .

MADELEINE: You've done that already!

AMÉDÉE: I'll go and roll him up . . .

MADELEINE: That won't stop him getting bigger. He's growing
in all directions at once! Where are we going to put him? What
are we to do with him? What's to become of us!

(pp. 177–8)

At first husband and wife assume the corpse is that of her lover
who was killed fifteen years ago, but the man soon knows
better.

AMÉDÉE: Was it really this young Romeo that we . . . that I
killed? It seems to me,–oh, what a memory I've got! . . . it seems
to me that the young man had already left . . . when the crime
was committed . . .

MADELEINE: If it's not the young man, who else could it possibly
have been?

AMÉDÉE: Perhaps it was the baby.

MADELEINE: The baby?

AMÉDÉE: A neighbour once asked us to look after a baby. Do you
remember? It was years ago. She never came to take it away . . .

(p. 188)

No specific deed is necessary for the birth of guilt.

AMÉDÉE: Now I come to think of it, I'm not sure it wasn't someone else . . .

MADELEINE: Who then? What are you getting at now?

AMÉDÉE: Listen . . . You know I was in the country one day
fishing . . . a woman fell in the water and shouted for help. As I
can't swim—and anyway the fish were biting—I stayed where I
was and left her to drown . . .

MADELEINE: And how would you explain the presence of this
corpse in our flat?

AMÉDÉE: Oh! . . . I don't know about that. It might have been
brought here for artificial respiration . . . Or it could have come
by itself . . .

(pp. 189–90)

When the corpse has at last filled both the rooms of the
apartment, Amédée and Madeleine make a determined effort
to get rid of it. And now it develops a strange beauty of its
own—the tragic beauty which belongs to humanity by virtue
only of guilt and frustration.

(. . . *suddenly strange music is heard coming from the dead man's
room and gradually growing louder . . . Amédée and Madeleine
listen in silence and without a movement in the deepening gloom;
which is gradually replaced by a green glow issuing from the
bedroom.*) (pp. 203–4)

MADELEINE: What's that? Do you hear? . . .

AMÉDÉE: . . . It's him, he's singing.

MADELEINE: But his mouth is shut. . . .

AMÉDÉE: I expect the sounds are coming out of his ears. . . . they're
the best musical instruments of all . . .

(*For a time there is nothing but the music, then the stage, which is
almost completely dark, is suddenly lit by a not unpleasant green
light that comes from the dead man's room . . .*)

MADELEINE: The light's coming from his room. That's where it's
coming from all right.

AMÉDÉE: It's his eyes shining . . . like tow beacons . . .

(pp. 204–5)

In this setting which 'must definitely suggest the mingled presence of horror and beauty', the corpse is at last manhandled out of the window.

> (*Amédée makes a supreme, a superhuman effort. He pulls very hard: once, twice, a third time, and then, suddenly, the body yields to him, with a tremendous crash that breaks the silence, as chairs are pulled over, plaster falls from the ceiling, clouds of dust rise and the whole set trembles. This should give the impression that as the body – its head still invisible – is steadily pulled nearer the window, it is dragging the whole set with it and tugging at the entrails of the two principal characters.*)

MADELEINE: Be careful, or he'll have all the china down . . .

AMÉDÉE: He'd really got rooted in the flat . . . He's so heavy . . . The strength of inertia! . . . He's harder to pull out than an old wisdom tooth . . . tougher than an oak.

(pp. 211–12)

When this apparently super-human effort has succeeded, and the flat is at last freed from the corpse, human life is over for Amédée, and he floats together with the corpse into the Empyrean, letting fall his shoes and cigarettes for the policeman and the soldiers with their molls wffo watch his mysterious ascent. Calling from mid-air he tries to explain but can only apologise!

AMÉDÉE: I'm terribly sorry. Please forgive me, Ladies and Gentlemen . . . Please don't think . . . I should like to stay . . . stay with my feet on the ground . . . It's against my will . . . I don't want to get carried away . . . I'm all for progress, I like to be of use to my fellow men . . . I believe in social realism . . . I wanted, I wanted to take the weight of the world on my shoulders.

(p. 225)

Such an ideal could be relied on to bestow a truly unbearable burden, but Amédée has escaped from it at last.

Forgive me, Ladies and Gentlemen, I'm terribly sorry! Forgive me! Oh, dear! But I feel so frisky, so frisky. (*He disappears.*)

(p. 226)

The weight of responsibility which will inevitably involve men with the weight of failure and of guilt appears to be essential for the life which we recognise as human, and, if this pattern were ever to be broken, life as we know it would end.

When Amédée has accepted his own act, wound its consequences round himself and become one with it, he becomes also free of the limitations of his human condition. He is airborne at last, but this fantasy of the integrated self still leaves a dichotomy unresolved. Acceptance of our own inadequacy is necessary if it is necessary to accept the truth, and when he has succeeded in doing this, Amédée is indeed carefree and 'frisky' in the upper air, but he is alone there. So long as man desires his brother's keeping he must be his brother's keeper, and Pim and Bom will continue their mutual torture and its fleeting assuagements. As O'Neill's Jamie reminded his brother, Oscar Wilde learnt truth not in the Empyrean heavens but in the yard of Reading Gaol!

> And all men kill the thing they love,
> By all let this be heard,
> Some do it with a bitter look,
> Some with a flattering word,
> The coward does it with a kiss,
> The brave man with a sword!*

For the artist there remains the task of finding a means of expression for this unending dilemma, and the expression can grow only from experience of the anguish. The kiss of Justice and Peace remains the compelling ideal but:

> Between the idea
> And the reality
> Between the motion
> And the act
> Falls the shadow.†

---

* *The Ballad of Reading Gaol*, 1898.

† T. S. Eliot, 'The Hollow Men', *Collected Poems 1909–1962*, Faber & Faber, 1963.

One last image of the human dilemma—the description in Thomas Mann's novel, *Dr. Faustus*,* of the music which its hero finally achieved not by coming to terms with his guilt but at the cost of accepting his own damnation.

At the end of this work of endless lamentation, softly, above the reason and with the speaking unspokenness given to music alone, it touches the feelings. I mean the closing movement of the piece . . . Here towards the end, I find . . . the final despair achieves a voice, and—I will not say it, it would seem to disparage the uncompromising character of the work, its irremediable anguish to say that it affords . . . any other consolation than what lies in voicing it, in simply giving sorrow words; in the fact, that is, that a voice is given the creature for its woe. But . . . listen to the end, listen with me: one group of instruments after another retires, and what remains, as the work fades on the air, is the high G of a cello, the last word, the last fainting sound slowly dying in a pianissimo-fermata. Then nothing more: silence, and night. But that tone which vibrates in the silence, which is no longer there, to which only the spirit hearkens, and which was the voice of mourning, is so no more. It changes its meaning; it abides as a light in the night.

* Secker & Warburg, 1949, pp. 490–1.

INDEX

Abel, divine vengeance on, 30
  as suffering servant, 187, 192
  blood of/innocent blood, 20,
    22–3, 26, 42, 130, 138, 146
Absurd/absurdity, 11, 14, 61, 69,
    79, 152
  absurd universe, 148–86
Albee, Edward
  Who's Afraid of Virginia
    Woolf?, 204–5
  Zoo Story, 201–4
Allen, Cardinal
  A Defence of Purgatory, 55
Aquinas, Thomas
  Summa Theologiae, 20
Arden, John
  Serjeant Musgrave's Dance,
    190–3
Arden of Faversham, 34
Atheist's Tragedy, The, 32
Athenian Drama, 11, 13–14
Augustine, St., 159

Bachofen, J. J., *see Kerygma and*
  Myth
Baldwin, James
  The Fire Next Time, 180
Baudelaire, C.
  Les Fleurs du Mal, 167
Beckett, Samuel, 139, 152 ff.
  All That Fall, 204
  Comment C'est, 154, 158–9,
    163–6, 167–8
  Endgame, 160
  Happy Days, 167
  Molloy, 160–3
  Play, 159, 167
  The Unnameable, 159
  Waiting for Godot, 139, 154–60
Berkeley, Bishop, 161
Bevan, E.
  Symbolism and Belief, 120

Bible, The
  Genesis (IV vv. 8–15), 15–16,
    47, 88
  Matthew (V v. 29), 156
  Romans (XII v. 19), 43
Brecht, Bertolt, 21–2, 59
  Baal, 21, 184–6
  Kuhle Wampe, 21
  Mother Courage, 24–6
Buber, Martin
  I and Thou, 163, 196, 203
Bultmann, Rudolf, *see Kerygma*
  and Myth
Bunyan, John
  The Pilgrim's Progress, 153
Byron, Lord
  Cain, 168

Cain and Abel, 12–13, 18–19,
    22–4, 56, 139, 158, 168–9,
    174, 187–9, 198, 201
  in *Genesis*, 15–16
  in medieval drama, 16–18
Cain, 49, 87–8, 123, 129, 137,
    164, 167, 168–9, 173
  as Antonio, 56
  as Coriolanus, 49
  as Edmund, 55
  as Iago, 46
  as Lear, 48–9
  as Macbeth, 18–19, 48
  descendants of, 180
  in works of Brecht, 185
    of Byron, 168
    of Ibsen, 88, 108, 114
    of Sartre, 137
    of Strindberg, 123, 129, 133
  mark of, 12, 138
  punishment/exile of, 13, 18,
    43, 47, 87, 133, 139, 146,
    184, 185
  See also Abel

217